JETPORT

Other Books by Dorothy Nelkin

Methadone Maintenance—A Technological Fix

The University and Military Research: Moral Politics at M.I.T.

The Politics of Housing Innovation: The Fate of the Civilian Industrial Technology Program

Nuclear Power and its Critics, The Cayuga Lake Controversy

Migrant: Farm Workers in America's Northwest (with William H. Friedland)

On the Season: Aspects of the Migrant Labor System

JETPORT:

The
Boston Airport Controversy

by
Dorothy Nelkin

ta

Transaction Books
New Brunswick, New Jersey

Copyright © 1974 by Transaction, Inc.
New Brunswick, New Jersey

(Library of Congress)   74-78-793
0-87855-591-9 (paper)
0-87855-111-5 (cloth)
Printed in the United States of America

CONTENTS

Tables

Abbreviations

AOCI	Airport Operators Council International
ATA	American Transport Association
BRA	Boston Redevelopment Agency
BTPR	Boston Transportation Planning Review
CAB	Civil Aeronautics Board
dB	decibel
DOD	Department of Defense
DOT	U.S. Department of Transportation
DPW	Department of Public Works
EPA	Environmental Protection Agency
EPNdB	Effective Perceived Noise in decibels
FAA	Federal Aviation Administration
GBC	Greater Boston Committee on the Transportation Crisis
HEW	U.S. Department of Health, Education and Welfare
HUD	U.S. Department of Housing and Urban Development
LANAC	Logan Airport Noise Abatement Committee
MAPC	Metropolitan Area Planning Council
MAPNAC	Massachusetts Air Pollution and Noise Abatement Committee
MBTA	Massachusetts Bay Transit Authority
NASA	National Aeronautics and Space Agency
NEF	Noise Exposure Forecast
NEPA	National Environmental Policy Act
NOISE	National Organization to Insure a Sound-Controlled Environment
OST	Office of Science and Technology
PIC	Boston Public Improvement Commission
STOL	Short Take-off and Landing Aircraft
USGPO	United States Government Printing Office
VTOL	Vertical Take-off and Landing Aircraft

Acknowledgments

Social research requires cooperation and assistance from many people. I am indebted to the Cornell University Program on Science, Technology and Society, an interdisciplinary program concerned with problems relating to the interaction of technology with society. Working daily with a staff including lawyers, economists, scientists and engineers, one is quickly sensitized to a broad range of problems and perspectives. More specifically, the staff members provided necessary criticism of technical details.

I am also indebted to many people from East Boston, Massport, Boston City Hall, the Office of State Transportation in Massachusetts, the Boston Transportation Planning Review and Bolt, Beranek and Newman. They provided documents, letters and transcripts of meetings and speeches as well as insight into the many facets of the Logan Airport controversy. In addition, most of the participants in the controversy submitted to long personal interviews. Alan Altshuler, James Fay, Peter Koff, Edward King, Richard Mooney and Albert Sallese were especially giving of their time, supplementing interviews with valuable unpublished material.

A number of people read and gave detailed and extensive criticism of an early draft. These include Alan Altshuler, Robert Behn, Phillip Bereano, David Edge, James Fay, Ralph Gakenheimer, Peter Koff, Arnim Meyburg, Robert Morison, Mark Nelkin, Marie Provine, Thomas Reiner, Fred Salvucci, Martin Sherwin and David Standley. The development of the study was also helped by discussion with two graduate students at Cornell, Barbara Robins and Sidney Siskin. As in the case of any controversial topic there is little agreement on the views expressed in any one analysis; responsibility naturally rests with the author alone.

I would also like to acknowledge the help of Helen Wolfers, who provided a daily newspaper clipping service for more than one year. Sidney Siskin edited the manuscript and Marjorie Kearl patiently typed it through many drafts. I am grateful to the National Science Foundation for supporting much of the research and writing.

INTRODUCTION: TECHNOLOGICAL CONTROVERSIES

Everywhere, symbols of progress are under attack. Technologies of speed and power—airports, electric power utilities, highways, dams—provoke bitter political antagonism as local communities protest against increasing burdens of noise, pollution and disruption. Great technological advances are invariably controversial; along with their benefits they generate distressing side effects, which have stimulated a growing tide of law suits, protests and demonstrations as various groups try to bring community values to bear on major technological decisions.

Technological controversies reflect several trends. First, side effects of technological development have become increasingly visible and disruptive, and concern with "the quality of life" is clearly seen to conflict with the tendency toward unconstrained growth. At the same time, changes in urban life have fostered resentment of bureaucracy and have increased demands for self-determination and local control. Heightened sensitivity to the environmental and social implications of modern technology has converged with disillusionment with the specialized institutions of a technological society. While public bureaucracies grow in order to cope with increasingly complex technology, there is widespread doubt about their credibility and political responsibility. Urban neighborhoods feel that patterns of technological development neglect to consider local needs and, as a result, apparently prosaic administrative issues such as the expansion of airports give rise to dramatic expression of community discontent. Thus, we see diverse groups—neighborhoods, clients, consumers— form coalitions around various issues in an effort to force authorities to be more responsive to their needs.[1]

The local social and environmental problems caused by the siting of a facility (such as a power plant or airport) and the demands of community-based citizens groups pose dilemmas for project developers. A project is often part of a large-scale regional system that calls for centralized planning and coordination. Decisions are usually made within large, specialized bureaucracies with few provisions for the involvement of citizen groups that may respond negatively to a project. The public hearings and information meetings set up to meet recent federal and state requirements for "citizen participation" often fail to satisfy disaffected groups. Such provisions for participation in the decision process have been at best token, but this is less a consequence of bureaucratic intent than of basic organizational arrangements. Specialized bureaucracies that develop technological projects function according to a formal system of rules and procedures designed to fulfill narrowly defined objectives. Decisions are made on the basis of specialized technical competence, and there is little tolerance for the uncertainty and unpredictability that wider citizen involvement is likely to introduce. Bureaucracies assume that their plans reflect a broad public consensus on the ultimate value of technological progress. They identify their actions with the public interest and seek to maintain their autonomy and remain insulated from the political process.[2]

In the past, with a supportive or at least acquiescent public, they were under little pressure to be accountable. As a matter of course, decisions about public technologies with far-reaching political and social implications were considered technical matters. But institutional authority increasingly has been challenged in a number of controversies across the United States, and bureaucratic structures are no longer inviolable. Community groups now place public agencies and private corporations under pressure for accountability. It is no longer enough for the managers of airports, utilities and other bureaucracies simply to plan. Large administrative organizations must win acceptance of their projects in the face of often bitter opposition based on values that they barely understand. In short, "people are just not willing to play by the old rules."[3]

Community-initiated controversies are invariably related to the distribution of costs and benefits. Developers of a project have a specific objective that they seek to reach in the most efficient way possible. Thus they work in terms of a calculus of efficiency that only incorporates costs that can be quantified. Persons whose lives are disrupted by a development define costs to include environmental and social impacts.[4] When decisions fail to reflect their values, such persons question the planning process itself, demanding "bureaucratic accountability" and greater participation and influence.

Opposition to technological projects develops in stages as public questions about specific issues are transformed into concern with the decision-making process.[5] An airport operator (or utility manager or developer) plans to expand a facility and applies for the necessary federal and state permits. Individuals or groups in the neighborhood try to prevent further action by complaining directly to the project developer, to regulatory agencies or to political representatives. They may try to block the entire project or demand specific changes. If normal political channels appear to be unresponsive, negative local reaction may assume the form of public meetings or demonstrations. Throughout, project managers claim that their plans, which are based on predictions of future needs and technical imperatives, are definitive except, perhaps, for minor adjustments necessary to meet federal regulations.

Citizen demonstrations attract national environmental groups, which join forces with local community activists. The project developer tries to allay their fears, but he usually does not respond directly to specific demands. This increases public opposition, and the situation may be polarized. Once a project becomes a matter of political debate, the problems raised by critics can no longer be ignored or dismissed as an inevitable and relatively minor cost of progress. As the issue becomes increasingly visible through the participation of national groups and the interest of the media, political leaders may intervene. Debate over technical data and their interpretation often takes place in public hearings. Particular problems are brought to court, but the uncompromising character of legal decisions (that they are either for or against a party) may lead to still further polarization.[6] Opponents of a technological project justify their position on moral grounds while the project planners claim a "rationality" not to be found in the "irrational" demands of the opposition. More well established than citizen groups, planners may also gain legitimacy through a legislative mandate or their obligations to bondholders. The situation is often seen as a choice between "people or progress." In the end, the values of economic development, with its implications for employment and general prosperity, often overwhelm competing values of community and environment. In some places, however, conflict has resulted in stalemate and projects have been indefinitely delayed.

The dynamics of technological controversy—the character of citizen pressure and the institutional response—will be analyzed in this study through the details of a particular conflict concerning airport development—a plan to expand Logan International Airport in Boston, Massachusetts. Disputes over airport planning are becoming increasingly frequent throughout the United States and the rest of the world. Long a source of pride, "the jewel in technology's crown," airports have become the subjects of intense debate, their expansion opposed by citizens groups, environmentalists, city planners and, increasingly, politicians. Airports that were built prior to the jet age are becoming congested just at a time when expansion is constrained by limited availability of land, serious complaints about noise and inadequate ground access.[7] Airport operators are caught between their involvement in a nationally coordinated system of airport planning and their immediate presence in particular neighborhoods, between client demands for expanded airport capacity and neighbors' concern with peace and quiet. Their decisions also affect environmental and land-use planning, housing and community development, public health, employment and location of industries. Many interests are thus touched in different ways by airport decisions, among them passengers and commercial users, bondholders, airport employees and construction workers, local business interests, the air transportation industry and adjacent neighborhoods. In short, airport development has profound implications for both the structure of economic development and the quality of life in an area. Furthermore, controversies concerning airport siting and expansion, which are taking place all over the world, have become an interorganizational problem involving relationships among municipal, state and federal governments, agencies and private interests.

These diverse perspectives are illustrated by the case of Logan Airport. To some 10 million passengers per year Logan, the eighth busiest airport in the world, is a modern, convenient facility. To its neighbors, however, Logan is a source of extreme irritation, fear and disruption. To city government, dependent on votes and income from taxable properties, the airport represents a political and economic problem. To state officials responsible for coordinating regional planning the airport is clearly an economic boon, but its expansion threatens to disrupt efforts to develop a balanced transportation system. Finally, to several national environmental groups the airport is a source of air and water pollution and a threat to Boston Harbor and the fish and wildlife of that area. Airport opponents may emphasize different problems, but all of them have raised fundamental questions about the values to be considered in decisions about public projects and about the control and accountability of institutions responsible for such decisions.

Since 1959, responsibility for Logan Airport has rested with the Massachusetts Port Authority (Massport). Massport, as a public authority, lies between the private and public sector. Established to operate in the public interest, it retains many of the rights and privileges of a governmental body. But its system of financing by revenue bonds, independent of state appropriations, allows it to operate much like a private business. Its responsibilities include Logan Airport, Hanscom Field (a small airport in Bedford, Massachusetts), the seaport and the Maurice J. Tobin (Mystic River) Bridge. Legally, Massport is permitted to focus narrowly on airport development and largely to ignore the impact of airport activities on neighboring communities. This arrangement, intended to expand New England's air-transportation service has been most efficient. However, Logan Airport is only two miles from downtown Boston and thus close to the heavily populated areas of East and South Boston, Winthrop, Chelsea and Revere. It is immediately adjacent to East Boston, an old working-class community of nearly 40,000 people. As the airport has expanded, this area has been affected by the noise of jet aircraft and by loss of real property. Although land-taking affects fewer people than noise, it raises even greater concern among airport neighbors who are fearful of having their lives disrupted and upset by the uncertainty about the future of their community.

Until the late 1960s, the equation of airport expansion with technological progress tended to divert public attention from its negative side effects. Noise and neighborhood disruption were acknowledged costs of jet transportation, but they were widely accepted as inevitable and unavoidable. When the East Boston community first raised issues that reflected values contradictory to those supporting technological growth—and those of the airport in particular—they were considered as politically insignificant.[8] In any case, the financial autonomy of Massport and the size and complexity of such a large-scale technological facility as Logan Airport discouraged political discussion of specific decisions.

By the end of the 1960s a conspicuous new pattern of criticism had developed in Boston reflecting the increasing tendency to question the narrow criteria used to justify many public activities. Massport was called "an octopus," and each time it threatened to extend its "cancerous tentacles" many East Bostonians reacted, demanding that the problems such expansion created for airport neighbors be included as a cost of airport development. Observing that the interests of East Boston had long been neglected as the airport expanded, they demanded redress of injury as a first order of business. Over the years, East Boston residents became increasingly well organized and politically effective.

Yet, despite articulate concern within neighboring communities, the controversial aspects of airport expansion did not become a serious political issue until around early 1970. During John Volpe's tenure as Governor of Massachusetts (1964 to 1969) he strongly supported airport expansion and worked to obtain federal funds and remove legislative obstacles. By 1969, however, community interests converged with increasing national sensitivity to problems associated with technological progress. For some years Boston had witnessed community concern about environmental and transportation problems, having been besieged by antihighway activists since the early 1960s. This activity culminated in 1970 when the governor of Massachusetts placed a moratorium on new highway construction and established the Boston Transportation Planning Review, a $3.5 million study project designed to develop an informed, coordinated transportation policy. That review attempted to make alternatives to each transportation decision available for political scrutiny in a framework that included participation by citizens as well as technical experts. Although this activity centered around highway construction, it has helped legitimate any questioning of technological policy that excludes social impact as a significant cost. Thus, it was politically viable by 1970 to assert that planners must consider the impact of airport development on community values and on local transportation systems. In this context the political leaders of East Boston were able to mobilize local citizens and gather support from several outside groups for their opposition to airport expansion.

But even when organized, such groups are relatively powerless when they oppose an airport authority supported by a major national industry and regional economic interests. Each time a runway extension or a new terminal building was proposed, Massport planners argued that airport expansion was inevitable and absolutely imperative for the health of the greater Boston economy. In each case the planners buttressed their position with technical justifications based on the advice of well-known consultants. However, opposing groups soon began mustering their own experts to deal with the technological complexities of the issue, and they presented recommendations reflecting quite different concerns. Mistrust precluded negotiation or even sustained dialogue between Massport and its critics.

After a conflict over a proposed new runway on July 8, 1971, Governor Francis W. Sargent publicly acknowledged the problem, stated his own opposition to the expansion plans for Logan Airport and set forth a philosophy that he thought should guide future airport planning. He recommended that expansion be deferred until studies determined the viability of alternatives that might minimize environmental impact. Subsequently, the governor tried to change the decision-making structure of Massport in order to force the authority to consider the overall transportation and community problems of greater Boston.

Massport's insistence on autonomy and the community's demand for participation in decisions affecting its interests reflects the inherent conflict between a bureaucracy's drive toward efficiency and the public's desire for political accountability.[9] This conflict inevitably raises serious and difficult questions. How can individuals or groups best approach public officials and powerful bureaucracies in order to force substantive changes in policies that affect their interests? The well-discussed limits of pluralist democracy in dealing with the basic demands of relatively powerless groups[10] are particularly problematic in technological areas where so many decisions require expertise. While it is now widely acknowledged that technological decisions must incorporate community values, the way to introduce these values into a context dominated by consultants and experts remains controversial.[11] How can institutions that, like Massport, are organized to minimize political influence in order to maximize economic efficiency respond to a political style of decision-making that in economic terms may be less efficient? Can elected officials or the courts control specialized bureaucracies without a critical loss of efficiency in the delivery of public services?[12]

Technological controversies also raise difficult questions

of social justice and minority rights—basic issues that have assumed new dimensions as technological change has rapidly outrun our decision-making apparatus.[13] Can the intense interests of 40,000 people who are exposed daily to the jet noise and the disruption caused by a major airport be measured against the convenience of millions of airport users? How can decisions take into account the fact that those who benefit from technology may not be those who bear the environmental costs? What are the grounds for negotiation when a broad, region-serving facility has only a localized impact?

This study will pursue such questions using the history of a particular case to explore the implications of increased citizen activity for the development of public policy concerning the location of technological facilities. In some ways the Logan Airport case is extreme; the airport's proximity to the city of Boston has exacerbated the problems related to airport operations, and the history of public concern with transportation planning in Boston has heightened the conflict. For our purposes, these extreme aspects of the case are useful. Conflict highlights the diverse interests and latent understandings that various groups bring to an issue and helps us analyze the political and organizational relationships that affect policy. It suggests both the advantages of the public authority structure and its limitations at times when its tasks become politically controversial. It exposes the dramatic intensity of community consciousness and the feeling of abandonment in the face of technological development. The case, then, is not presented as typical of airport controversies but rather as a set of events that reveals the rich network of issues influencing public decisions. The story touches on many problems that have been subject to detailed analysis elsewhere: the effects of noise on man, urban politics and community power, relationships among state, federal and municipal governments, problems of bureaucratic rationality and decision-making, the role of the courts in technol-

ogical areas and philosophical questions concerning conflicting values and social justice. This analysis will suggest
how these issues influence the development of policy in a
specific area. Footnotes will refer the reader to the related
analytic literature.

In Part 1 the background to airport controversies will be
presented, along with an account of the problems posed by
the development of jet technology and the existing mechanisms of regulation and control. In Part 2, after a brief
history of Logan Airport and its administration, the
airport's local impact and the community's reaction will be
analyzed in the context of specific efforts by airport
neighbors to constrain the activities of the airport administration. Part 3 will analyze the response of city and state
officials and their attempts to intervene in the decision-
making of a politically autonomous public authority. This
is followed in Part 4 by a discussion of Massport's mix of
symbolic and substantive accommodations to political
pressure. Finally, the Boston airport controversy will be
used to analyze some of the tensions inherent in policies
concerning technological change.

Part I: AIRPORT CONTROVERSIES

1
PROBLEMS OF AIRPORT DEVELOPMENT

The airplane has long been a focus of opposition as well as acclaim. Legal complaints about aircraft noise since the first suit in 1928 have included cracked plaster, dead mink, damaged eggs, sterile chickens and distraught families.[1] Judicial opinion has had a confused history, muddled by the ambiguous concept of "air space," ambivalent perspectives on "progress" and the changing dimension of the problem with the development of modern jet technology. Airport activity has become increasingly controversial since the introduction of commercial jet aircraft in 1958. Jets make more noise and require longer runways and more clear land than piston-engine planes. As commercial aviation has converted to jet technology (see Table 1), problems of noise and land-use planning have often provoked violent responses from neighboring communities. Political and regulatory institutions have sought to control such reactions, but jetports remain among the most controversial of modern technological facilities.

PUBLIC OPPOSITION

Initially, public opposition to airport noise focused on the air force, the first user of jet aircraft, but it was usually dismissed on grounds of patriotism. "What would happen if our boys were not up there?" Opposition to noise from commercial airports began in 1959 with the beginning of public jet service. At that time, a citizen protest stopped airport operations for several days at Idlewild (now Kennedy) Airport in New York. Subsequently, airports throughout the world have been besieged by complaints, petitions, lawsuits, demonstrations and sometimes violent threats.

TABLE 1
Commercial Aircraft

	2&3-Engine Turbo-Fan	4-Engine Turbo-fan	4-Engine Wide-body Turbofan	3-Engine Wide-body Turbofan	Pro-peller Air-craft
Aircraft Identi-fication	B727, B737, DC-9 BAC-111	B707, B720, DC-8	B747	DC-10, L-1011	F27, CV 340/440, DC-3
Passenger Capacity	100	150	365	250	40
Noise at 1,000 ft. (dB)					
Approach	85-90	94-100	92	84	75-82
Take-off	94-100	100-105	103	90	85-90
Number of Aircraft					
1960	0	202	0	0	1,640
1970	1,174	815	79	0	380

Source: U.S. Environmental Protection Agency, "Transportation Noise and Noise from Equipment Powered by Internal Combustion Engines," NTID 300-13, Washington, D.C., December 31, 1971.

TABLE 2
Air Traffic Activity at FAA Facilities, by Aviation Category
(Fiscal Years 1961-1971)

Fiscal Year	Total Number of Operations	Annual Change (%)	Air Carrier Number of Operations	Annual Change (%)	General Aviation Number of Operations	Annual Change (%)	Military Number of Operations	Annual Change (%)
1961	25,623,718	−3	6,969,367	−5	14,925,312		3,729,039	−8
1962	27,415,418	+7	7,147,920	+3	16,422,055	+10	3,845,443	+3
1963	29,190,087	+6	7,105,560	−1	18,396,369	+12	3,688,158	−4
1964	32,857,745	+13	7,444,238	+5	21,618,306	+18	3,795,201	+3
1965	35,557,868	+8	7,513,643	+1	24,431,036	+13	3,613,189	−5
1966	41,209,592	+16	8,191,768	+9	29,694,994	+22	3,322,830	−8
1967	47,584,327	+15	8,563,698	+5	35,711,625	+20	3,309,004	
1968	52,998,583	+11	9,881,300	+15	39,766,572	+11	3,350,711	+1
1969	55,890,476	+5	10,713,216	+8	41,811,152	+5	3,366,108	
1970	56,181,465	+1	10,807,901	+1	42,012,008		3,361,556	
1971	54,249,954	−3	10,063,387	−7	40,667,851	−3	3,518,716	+5

Source: Department of Transportation, Federal Aviation Administration, *Air Traffic Activity,* Washington, D.C., 1971.

The airport system expanded rapidly during the 1960s, slowing down only in response to a general economic decline in 1970 (see Table 2).[2] In 1972 airport planners were assuming that airline passenger traffic would continue to increase at an average annual rate of 10 percent. Former FAA administrator John Shaffer predicted that 1,000 new airports would be needed by 1982, 100 of which would be for commercial airline use.[3] By the beginning of 1974, fuel shortages and a growing sense of economic uncertainty caused a major decline in air traffic. Airports in the New York area, for example, had 23-percent fewer flights in January 1974 than in January 1973. Community groups opposed to airport development argue that this calls for major reassessment of jetport expansion needs.

The Kansas City Airport, opened in 1972, and the Dallas-Fort Worth Airport, opened in 1973, are the only new airports to be built since 1969, and both were started prior to that date. Given the level of organized opposition, these two new airports may be the last built for many years to come. Opposition recently prompted the president of the American Association of Airline Executives to predict that, "We will probably have to go with what we have now to 1980."[4] And in January 1973 the Aviation Advisory Commission (appointed by Congress to conduct a two-year study on the future of aviation) criticized plans for new airports that failed to reflect the relationship between air travel and other activities in urban areas. They recommended a dispersed airport system and proposed pricing incentives for more efficient use of existing airport facilities.[5]

Airport operators throughout the world are faced with political and legal battles that have blocked new airport construction in nearly every major city and have delayed the expansion of older pre-jet-age airports built close to heavily populated areas. Los Angeles Airport was initially built with considerable room for expansion. It now faces over $5 billion in damage suits; its management hopes to avoid additional suits by buying up surrounding property at about $340,000 an acre, and since 1968 it has spent more than $200 million moving or razing homes along airport boundaries.

In Florida, the Dade County Port Authority purchased a 38-square-mile site in the Everglades far from developed areas, inhabited chiefly by alligators. They built a small military training strip and in 1969 received FAA funds to expand. Conservationists concerned with the loss of a major natural resource successfully prevented the development of the commercial airport, arguing that land-use decisions affecting national parks such as the Everglades should not be left to local authorities. Two reports appeared—one funded by the Port Authority, the other by the Department of the Interior—and they disagreed as to the potential damage. Governor Claude Kirk finally intervened and the site was rejected. A second Florida site, 15 miles northwest of Miami, was successfully opposed by civic organizations and condominium owners because of anticipated noise and traffic congestion.

At Dulles Airport in Washington, D.C., citizens are suing the FAA, which occupies a dual role as airport regulator and airport operator, for violating Fairfax County zoning regulations.

In Palmdale, California, residents opposed a desert airport because of the industrial development that would follow and change the character of the area.

In New York, the siting of a fourth jetport has been controversial since the first proposal for a site in Morris County, New Jersey, was made in 1959. Subsequent proposals for a jetport in the lower bay of New York Harbor, at McGuire Air Force Base, on south-central Jersey's Pine Barrens, at Solberg Airport in Readington, New Jersey, and at 22 other sites were studied and rejected after opposition by local residents and ecologists. Political organization, protest marches and demonstrations have occurred whenever a site is proposed and the issue has become a factor in New Jersey political campaigns. As a result the Port Authority contracted a National Academy of Sciences committee to study the environmental impact of extending Kennedy Airport, hoping to work with ecologists to avoid controversy. But the committee opposed expansion and recommended changes in operating procedures to relieve congestion. The most recent proposal, also controversial, is Stewart Airport in Newburgh, New York, 65 miles from Manhattan. Meanwhile a $400 million expansion and redevelopment program at Newark Airport was completed in 1973 despite a long history of concern in that heavily populated area about noise and community safety. Three crashes in 1951 and 1952 had forced a temporary closing of the airport. Airport neighbors demanded that the airport be moved, but the Port Authority remained undaunted and, since then, Newark Airport has more than doubled its operations.

The United States is not alone with its difficulties in developing and expanding airports. In London, administrators received 2,200 complaints in 1969 about the noise generated by Heathrow Airport and put aside plans to increase the airport's capacity by adding a third major runway. The initial plan to expand an airport at Stansted was rejected because of concerted local opposition that included proposals for military opposition with homemade molotov cocktails and gasoline bombs. The Roskill Commission was established in 1968 in an effort to reach a systematic decision based on extensive public participation. A series of public hearings and studies continued for several years, as all proposals were resisted by farmers, conservationists, suburbanites and villagers. A site was finally selected at Foulness on the North Sea, where a relatively poor and unorganized population raised little opposition. While selection of this site appeared to be politically expedient, 11,000 acres of land have to be reclaimed from the sea and a major railway access line has to be built. This airport (called Maplin), the largest development project ever conceived by the British Government, would cost £1,000 million. Yet there remains considerable question of whether, with the development of wide-bodied jets such as the 747, the third airport is necessary to accommodate increased air traffic. After considerable discussion, the plan is back in committee.[6]

Attempts to acquire land for an airport near Tokyo failed when farmers and students allied to physically block construction equipment. During the battles over this siting decision several policemen were killed and hundreds of students injured.[7]

In Copenhagen, a site for a new airport was finally approved after several alternatives were rejected following citizen-group protest actions. However, the new site, Saltholm, has become controversial because its noise corridor extends over Sweden, violating the country's stringent noise regulations. Near Stockholm a new town, Märsta, was developed in the early 1960s to serve Arlanda Airport. The town was located, on the basis of noise and land-use calculations, so as to be spared from noise disruption. But with advancing jet technology and increasingly stringent compatible land-use requirements, the old zoning regulations have become obsolete. Now Märsta, with its new housing development, lies within a critical noise zone. New town residents are bringing suit.[8]

And in Munich, a local citizen built a Roman ballista, loaded it with potato dumplings and fired it at low flying jets, successfully persuading the airport administration to change flight patterns.

The translation of individual annoyance into organized group opposition depends on many social and political factors in addition to the actual level of noise. Unless there is an active political group to organize public demonstrations or legal actions, relatively few people who are troubled by noise actually complain.[9] There is, however, an epidemiological effect, and the success of opposition groups in one area encourages similar activity elsewhere. The extent of antiairport activity depends on community leadership, patterns of neighborhood interaction, public attitudes toward the existing system of regulation, the presence of related threats such as land acquisition and the success of opposition elsewhere.[10] Organized communities attempt to dramatize their objections through petitions, demonstrations, physical obstruction and other actions that capture the attention of the media and otherwise influence legislators. In some cases, these groups engage their own experts to provide evidence to support their case and use national environmental issues to reinforce their local complaints.[11]

Success in influencing airport decisions may depend upon a community's ability to interest regional and national groups in its problem.[12] With an increasing number of controversies, national environmental associations are mobilized to assist local groups. The United States now has a national organization concerned specifically with airport noise, the National Organization to Insure a Sound-controlled Environment (NOISE), formed in 1968. Its original membership was from groups that had formed to oppose airport plans in Newark, Los Angeles, Chicago and Minneapolis. NOISE now includes some 30 groups, mostly from middle-class suburbs, who want the public authority or core-city management of airports to be responsive to the needs of suburban communities, which are most affected by airport activities. Primarily an educational organization, NOISE works with regulatory agencies and informally lobbies in Congress for noise legislation, hoping to set up more effective policies for the regulation of airport noise.

NOISE

Noise, often defined as "sound without value,"[1][3] is a waste product just like sewage or sludge. It is an increasing problem in urban areas, and transportation is its major source (see Table 3). As jet aircraft increased in number during the 1960s they became the most disturbing type of

TABLE 3
Transportation Noise
(1970)

Category	Number of vehicles in U.S.	Noise Level* dB (A scale)
Aircraft (Take-off Only)		
4-engine turbofan	894	103
2- and 3-engine turbofan	1,174	96
General Aviation	128,900	77
Helicopters	16	83
Highway Vehicles (add 000)		
Medium and heavy-duty trucks	3,640	84
Passenger cars (standard)	64,000	69
Light trucks and pickups	15,300	72
Motorcycles (highway)	2,600	82
City and school buses	380	73
Recreational Vehicles (add 000)		
Minicycles, off-road motorcycles	1,000	88
Snowmobiles	1,600	85
Outboard motorboats	5,200	75

Source: U.S. Environmental Protection Agency, "Transportation Noise and Noise from Equipment Powered by Internal Combustion Engines," NITD 300.13, Washington, D.C., December 31, 1971, Appendix B-3.

*Distance in feet from source of noise is 1,000 for aircraft and 50 for all others.

transportation noise, affecting large numbers of people living or working near airports. A jet engine produces the thrust necessary to push an aircraft by sucking in air and raising the temperature and air pressure inside the engine so that gases expand and are expelled with high velocity. Jet noise is primarily caused by the turbulent mixing of the high velocity exhaust with the surrounding air, and the noise is greatest during take-off. But, in addition, turbofan engines generate a high-frequency whine that is dominant during the landing approach.

There have been efforts to define "acceptable" levels of noise, though there is no scientifically precise way to measure its many effects or to predict the response of individuals or communities to unwanted sound. Sound is measured in decibels (dB), a unit that describes the intensity of the sound relative to a standard, usually equal to the lowest volume ordinarily detectible to the human ear. The decibel scale is logarithmic, so that an increase of three decibels represents a two-fold increase in sound intensity.[14] However, the perceived increase in loudness will be less than the actual increase in intensity, for the human perception of noise is also influenced by such factors as its duration, its spectrum (noise frequencies and pitch) and sudden changes in noise levels. In many ways decibels are to sound as degrees are to temperature; they measure magnitude but not human perception.

Only since the late 1960s has noise been widely recognized as a serious public health problem as well as an annoying pollutant.[15] Experiments suggest that excessive exposure to noise over a long period of time can cause permanent hearing loss. It has also been found that noise affects the autonomic nervous system, which controls involuntary functions of the heart, blood vessels and other internal organs.[16] Noise is also related to anxiety and nervous tension and therefore may affect work and school performance. And noise makes communication difficult.[17]

An environmental study of Jamaica Bay in New York, reports that 220 schools (attended by 280,000 pupils) close to Kennedy Airport are subject to about one hour's interruption each day because of the "jet pause" necessary each time an aircraft passes overhead.[18]

Laboratory tests indicate that the personal stress and interference with work associated with noise may be influenced by a number of cognitive factors that are impossible to measure with precision. An individual's feeling of "deprivation" when he perceives that he has to endure more noise than other people, his attitude toward the source of noise, his sense of control over it and the extent to which his concern is shared by others in his community all affect his reaction and therefore his tendency to complain or take legal action.[19]

TABLE 4
Land Use Compatibility for Aircraft Noise

Land-Use Compatibility	Noise Exposure Forecast Areas		
	Less than 30 NEF	Exposure to Between 30 and 40 NEF	Greater than 40 NEF
Residential	yes	(A)	no
Commercial	yes	yes	(B)
Offices, Public Buildings	yes	(B)	no
Schools, Hospitals, Churches	(B)	no	no
Outdoor Recreation	yes	yes	yes
Industrial	yes	yes	(B)

Source: Peter A. Franken et al., *Aircraft Noise and Aircraft Neighbors*, (Cambridge, Massachusetts: Bolt, Beranek and Newman, March 1970).

Note (A): Individuals in private residences may complain. New single-dwelling construction should generally be avoided.

Note (B): Needed noise-control features should be included in the building design.

Despite the difficulties in assessing the stress associated with noise there is a widely accepted technique used to predict community response, the Noise Exposure Forecast (NEF). In order to estimate a community's future exposure to noise, the noise configurations of the aircraft involved are measured; then, the expected frequency and distribution of daily air traffic are considered along with the general profile and paths of flights in an area. These data are combined and contours of "equal noise exposure" are drawn around an airport for the purpose of determining what land uses would be compatible with projected future annual average noise exposures.[20] Although NEF cannot adequately consider psychological and socio-economic variables that affect individual or community response to noise, it is the best tool available.

Federal guidelines based on this technique recommend that residential construction be avoided in areas exposed to more than NEF 30 (see Table 4). By 1970, however, this exposure was already exceeded in the United States in about 1,450 square miles, populated by 7.5 million people. About 47,000 dwelling units near Los Angeles Airport and 35,000 units near Kennedy are in high-noise zones. Ironically, the very existence of better air transportation encourages industrial growth near airports which in turn fosters the development of new residential communities.[21] Thus, the number of residential areas close to airports has tended to increase despite recognition of the noise problem. For example, a remarkable proposal to build a 24-square-mile island on Lake Erie for an international jetport included plans for an industrial complex and a new community of 200,000 people. At the same time that the city of San Francisco was suing the airport operator for $3.4 million for noise damages, it was also issuing building permits for new residential areas near the airport.

AIRPORTS AND CITY PLANNING

While noise is the most obvious issue associated with airports, other problems are significant, particularly in metropolitan areas. The expansion of commercial aviation coincided with the rapid growth of the suburbs, leading to competition for the rural land near large cities that is attractive both for airport and for residential use.[22] Airport expansion may be in direct competition with other plans for urban development, since both suburbanization and the movement of urban industry to locations outside central cities have limited the availability of open land areas.

As aircraft operations increase, access to airports becomes another troublesome issue that brings airport operators in direct conflict with those agencies of state and city government concerned with ground transportation. Most airline employees, passengers and visitors use private automobiles, and peak airport demands coincide with commuter rush hours. The introduction of wide-bodied jets has caused further congestion; a single 747 can attract up to 800 people to an airport at the same time. Highway planners worry that it will be financially and politically impossible to develop enough freeways to cope with the airport-access problem.[23] Yet airport planners design terminals and parking areas on the assumption that private automobile traffic will continue to increase. A survey of ground access at 23 major city airports throughout the world found that only four had direct rapid-transit rail service directly to an airport terminal building. Airport operators argue that the dispersed origin and destination points of airport users preclude successful alternative forms of transportation. They acknowledge the problem of congestion, but they see the solution in highway improvement rather than the development of rail or bus transit.[24]

Airport operators also are skeptical of proposals for decentralized terminals using bus or limousine transportation, anticipating problems from multiple baggage handling and uncertain airline departure times contingent on bus schedules. They doubt that passengers and airline employees could in fact be lured away from their private cars. Thus, airport operators have tended to view airport planning as an isolated issue, separable from the entire urban transportation system. City and state planners, however, are extremely concerned about both noise and highway congestion caused by ground access to airports. Along with federal agencies, they, too, attempt to influence the development, siting and operation of airports.

POLICIES

2

A growing tide of litigation and increasing political turmoil stimulated congressional interest during the 1960s and gradually forced changes in federal policy. Congress first became involved in airport issues in 1959 when a subcommittee of the House Interstate and Foreign Commerce Committee, chaired by Representative Oren Harris, began a series of hearings in response to complaints about Idlewild Airport. The Harris Committee hearings extended over several years and reported that federal noise-abatement legislation would not be useful given the importance of the economic health of the aviation industry and the inadequate scientific basis on which to set noise standards. Legislators, however, continued to be pressured by their constituents in noise-impacted areas, and the issue stayed alive as noise-abatement bills were repeatedly introduced into Congress. The most comprehensive of these bills, presented in 1966, would have established an Office of Noise Control in the surgeon general's office and would have centralized aviation-noise research in NASA. The bill failed to pass as did a later effort to earmark $20 million of NASA's budget authorization for quiet-engine research.

But in October 1965, a science advisor to President Lyndon B. Johnson named Donald Hornig created a jet aircraft noise panel that recommended increased federal government initiative in solving the problems of jet noise and a comprehensive program that would include research into new technology, new operating procedures and ways to influence compatible land-use planning. Increased federal recognition of the problem led, in 1968, to the establishment of an interagency aircraft noise-abatement program and an amendment to the 1968 Federal Aviation Act (Public Law 90—411) authorizing the FAA to develop standards and regulations for the measurement and control of aircraft noise. These regulations have formed the basis of current federal policy regulating aircraft noise.

REGULATION AND CONTROL

A formidable system of laws and regulations guides airport operations and ensures consideration of the environmental and social effects of all development plans. The system involves municipal, state and federal agencies and both public and private bureaucracies. The immediate responsibility belongs to the airport management, which in some cases is a public authority and in others is a commission run directly by the city or county government (see Table 5). Airport managers serve essentially as middle-men between the airlines and passengers—coordinating airport activities, dealing with local problems and building and maintaining runways and terminal buildings at a level consistent with demand. Because they are the focus of local pressure, airport managers are extremely aware of noise and land-use problems in neighboring communities, but their responsibilities lead them to view these adverse effects of airport expansion as inevitable and unavoidable costs of progress, costs that are outweighed by the direct

TABLE 5

20 Largest U.S. Air Carrier Airports: Size and Management (1970)

Airport	Enplaned Passengers (millions)	Airport Area (sq. miles)	Airport Management
Chicago (O'Hare)	13.5	14.1	City Department of Aviation
Los Angeles	8.5	4.8	City Board of Airport Commissioners
Atlanta	8.2	6.6	City of Atlanta
J.F. Kennedy	7.0	8.1	Port Authority of New York & New Jersey
La Guardia	5.9	0.9	Port Authority of New York & New Jersey
San Francisco	5.5	8.1	City and County Department of Aviation
Dallas (Love)	5.3	2.0	Dallas-Fort Worth Airport Commission (Authority)
Washington (Nat.)	4.9	1.0	FAA (National Capital Airport)
Boston	4.5	3.7	Massachusetts Port Authority
Miami	4.4	4.2	Dade County Port Authority
Detroit	3.7	7.5	City of Detroit Aviation Commission
Denver	3.5	7.2	City and County of Denver
Newark	3.4	3.4	Port Authority of New York and New Jersey
Philadelphia	3.2	3.9	City Division of Aviation
St. Louis	3.1	2.9	St. Louis Airport Authority
Pittsburgh	3.0	4.8	Allegheny County Department of Aviation
Minneapolis	2.6	4.6	City Airport Commission (Authority)
Cleveland	2.5	2.3	City of Cleveland
Seattle	2.5	2.8	Port of Seattle Commission (Authority)
Houston	2.2	11.4	City of Houston

benefits of airport development. They see expansion plans as meeting their public obligation to prevent saturation of existing facilities, and they argue that limitations on their operations would jeopardize safety and convenience.

The airlines control the scheduling of flights, but they do so within constraints imposed by the Civil Aeronautics Board (CAB) and the Federal Aviation Administration (FAA), which is now a part of the Department of Transportation (DOT). The CAB controls the routing of flights and also regulates the economics of interstate and international air traffic through control of fares and tariffs. While its economic leverage gives the agency potentially significant power to control jet noise, it is seldom drawn into controversies concerning environmental impacts.

The FAA, created in 1958 to encourage civil aeronautics, is responsible for air-traffic control, for regulating the use of runways and airways and for setting performance standards, particularly with respect to air safety. The agency has some control of areas outside the airport through its requirement that there be a "clear zone" with no physical obstructions beyond the runway. The FAA also limits the allowable noise level of new types of subsonic aircraft, making this a condition of certification.[2] The 1968 amendments to the Federal Aviation Act gave the FAA authority to fix standards for the measurement of aircraft noise and to set regulations for noise control and abatement. Using this authority, in November 1969 the FAA set maximum noise levels for new types of jet aircraft that would significantly reduce the noise from landings and take-offs of those planes subject to the regulation.

Environmental standards are subject to review under the National Environmental Policy Act (NEPA) of 1969. NEPA established environmental protection as a national policy. Before funding or approving any project (ranging from new airports to new aprons) federal agencies—

including the FAA—must submit a detailed environmental impact statement to the Council on Environmental Quality. The statement must include an evaluation of all potential environmental impacts, an account of unavoidable adverse affects and a list of alternatives to the proposed action.

Several months after NEPA was signed, Congress passed the Airport and Airway Development Act of 1970. This act requires airport projects needing federal aid to meet federal air and water quality standards.

Under the act the secretary of transportation must, in developing a comprehensive national airport plan, consult and wherever possible follow the recommendations of the Departments of Interior and Agriculture, HEW and the Council for Environmental Quality. The act also requires that airport development projects consider and be "reasonably consistent" with the plans of other agencies responsible for the development of an area. Thus, airport operators must conduct public hearings to evaluate social and environmental effects of airport location and to ensure that airport plans are consistent with other urban plans.

The FAA's primary concern is that airport operations be safe, efficient and compatible with its long-range goals for an integrated and expanded national airport system. As public concern about environmental and noise problems increases, the FAA's authority over noise regulations has been seriously questioned. The FAA, according to one critic, "establishes standards at levels slightly below that at which people complain vigorously, and this keeps the public sullen but not mutinous."[3] Similarly, others accuse the agency of "massive nonfeasance," of "talking out of both sides of its bureaucratic mouth in such a way to declare itself all-powerful or powerless, depending on which best suits the airport operators."[4] Concerned with the FAA's traditional orientation to the needs of industry and its commitment to the growth of commercial aviation,

Senator Alan Cranston (D-California) presented a bill to Congress in October 1971 that would have shifted control of noise impact from the FAA to the Office of Noise Abatement and Control within the Environmental Protection Agency (EPA). This office had been authorized by the Clean Air Act of 1970 to determine causes of noise and their effects on public health and to recommend to Congress long-range noise control and abatement programs. Senator Cranston's proposal was strongly opposed by CAB Chairman Secor Browne on the grounds that noise issues were linked to safety and that only the FAA was competent in this area. The issue was postponed for a year, and in October 1972 the Senate Public Works Committee considered a compromise bill introduced by Senators John Tunney (D-California) and Edmund Muskie (D-Maine) that would have given the EPA power to establish permissible noise-emission levels based on public health considerations. Both the FAA and the EPA would decide how noise controls would be implemented, taking into account cost, safety and technological feasibility. The bill, opposed by the American Transport Association (ATA) and the airline industry was turned down by Congress, concerned that: "Safety in the air is one of the things that must be given absolute priority."[5] Thus, when the Noise Control Act of 1972 gave EPA authority to set standards for consumer products that were identified as major sources of noise, it specifically excluded aircraft. Ultimate control of the aircraft noise problem remains within the FAA, which can reject environmental regulations if it believes they are "unsafe, technologically or economically unfeasible or not applicable to certain aircraft."[6] The FAA then issued a paper on its own policies concerning the environmental impact of airports.[7] This states that, "Environmental amenities and values are to be given careful and timely consideration and appropriate weight in all Federal airport planning and development decisions." FAA requirements are comprehensive; environmental values include impacts on social, economic and community development as well as noise and pollution. The required environmental report must include a statement that there are "no feasible and prudent alternatives to the proposed action; and further, the proposed action includes all possible steps to minimize harm to the environment." Yet it is the proponents of airport projects who must give "appropriate, complete, *objective* and timely consideration to environmental factors."[8] Furthermore, FAA criteria for evaluating these factors are necessarily vague; the policy statement observes, for example, that "significant effects on the quality of the human environment . . . [are] not subject to precise definition or a description of every possible circumstance."

Other agencies such as the Department of Housing and Urban Development (HUD) are involved in noise abatement only indirectly through control over federal aid to housing in airport-impacted areas. NASA conducts research programs on technology to "retrofit," that is, to install redesigned engines with lower noise output and to develop a "quiet engine."

The federal intention is to set up a single interagency unit to coordinate all the aircraft noise-abatement programs. But the regulatory structure is complex; the locus of responsibility in any specific situation is difficult to determine, and, as will be made evident in our discussion of the Boston airport situation, complexity often permits local authorities to deny their ability to respond to public demands and to "pass the buck" to federal agencies.

Federal regulations on noise normally override regulations at the local and state level. There are more than 1,200 noise ordinances in the United States ranging from a ruling in Philadelphia in 1830 outlawing the use of horns by street vendors to recent efforts to impose night curfews on airports. Many of these rulings are preempted by federal legislation. For example, the FAA has set up safety regulations requiring aircraft to fly at a certain height, and a city government cannot change that requirement.[9] However, federal rulings do not entirely preclude lawmaking by local and state governments. With the exception of the constraints established by HUD through its control of federal aid to housing, authority over compatible land-use planning and zoning largely remains with state and municipal governments. Local governments have often interpreted this to include authority over noisy aircraft. For example, the town of Hempstead, New York, passed an ordinance to forbid the operation of any mechanism (including airplanes) that would cause "unnecessary noise." Hempstead was sued by nine airlines, the Port Authority of New York and the administrator of the FAA. A federal court ruled that municipal ordinances of this sort are invalid because they are preempted by federal legislation.[10] In another case, a state court supported a municipal ordinance in Santa Monica, California, restricting the time of day when jets could take off from an airport.[11] But more recently in Burbank, California, a city ordinance prohibiting night flights was held unconstitutional by both a district court and the Court of Appeals on grounds of federal preemption.[12] The case was brought to the Supreme Court, which reaffirmed FAA control by ruling (in a 5-4 vote) that municipalities could not create local curfews.

Although night curfews cannot be established locally, airport operators are able to restrict the number of planes using an airport and, in response to community pressure, several operators in California have done so despite contrary economic pressures. They can also negotiate with FAA air controllers and pilots concerning ground operating procedures and runway use. Thus, in practice, a great deal of responsibility for determining permissible noise levels in areas near airports rests with airport operators, who apply federal standards to local conditions, coordinate federal regulations with municipal and state land-use ordinances and respond to specific community demands.[13]

NOISE-ABATEMENT POLICIES

The fight against noise pollution is waged on four fronts: adapting the existing technology of aircraft engines, designing new technological alternatives, changing aircraft operations and insulating or removing affected parties.[14]

Technological Adaptations

A promising method of reducing the noise of jet engines is to treat the nacelle, or engine casing, with a sound-absorbent lining. On November 12, 1969, the FAA ruled that new types of aircraft would be permitted a maximum noise level of 108 EPNdB (existing aircraft produced up to 120 EPNdB).[15] Although the new rules do not apply to existing aircraft or to some new types of aircraft such as the B727, they have stimulated considerable research to develop retrofit techniques for current turbofan engines. The FAA, for example, sponsored a 15-month, $7 million program to retrofit the Boeing 707. Tested in May 1973, the modified aircraft engine reduced noise by 10-15 decibels.

Technological solutions are appealing both to those affected by noise as well as to airport operators who bear the brunt of adverse public reaction and feel themselves caught between the airline industry and belligerent communities. However, the airline industry itself, concerned about costs and competition, considers the benefits of retrofit exaggerated. The general manager of Boeing claims, "There can be no doubt that it is not economically feasible to significantly change our older aircraft. They must live out their amortization life and eventually be retired."[16] "Invention cannot be scheduled," said a vice-president of American Airlines who also claimed that the present retrofit technology is too costly to be acceptable. Furthermore, airline executives feel that costly noise-reduction programs would not in any case significantly reduce complaints because airport opponents are politically motivated.

While the question of economic feasibility is controversial, the Airport Operators Council supports congressional legislation requiring airlines to retrofit their engines and contends that the entire fleet could be retrofitted for $1 billion, whereas dealing with the noise problem through land acquisition in airport areas would cost more than $50 billion.[17] EPA claims that the cost of retrofitting would be several billion dollars, a cost still significantly lower than other means of reducing noise.[18] In view of the reluctance of airlines to pay for engine modifications, the Federal Aviation Advisory Commission study panel appointed by Congress recommended that funds from the Airport Airways Trust Fund, normally used for airport construction, be diverted to airline companies for purposes of retrofitting their older planes.[19]

Technological Innovations and Alternatives

In addition to adapting existing engine systems, there are attempts to develop new types of jet engines specifically designed to reduce the problem of noise. Furthermore, the dual problem of noise and the limited availability of land for airport expansion has stimulated a search for alternative means of domestic intercity travel. One alternative is to develop high-speed rail transportation for the large number of airport passengers on the East Coast who fly relatively short distances. (In 1970, for example, 47 percent of all passengers at Boston's Logan Airport flew to New York City or Washington, D.C.) An advanced rail system similar to the Tokaido line in Japan with a top speed of 126 miles per hour or a tracked air-cushion vehicle system would require a new right-of-way in most areas, and it would also seriously compete with air transportation for distances up to 500 miles.[20]

Another alternative is to develop an aircraft technology that would permit a dispersed city airport system. NASA has awarded contracts to develop STOL and VTOL (short and vertical take-off and landing) aircraft which are intended to substitute for conventional aircraft on short runs up to 500 miles. They use propellors, jets or rotors to produce aerodynamic lift, plus conventionally mounted engines for normal cruising, and they need little or no runway space. A STOL aircraft is designed with four jet engines and a special system of flaps that deflect the jet exhaust downward to produce vertical thrust. The Canadian Transport Ministry has developed an 11-passenger model; commercial-size planes are expected to be airborne by 1975. They will require only 1,500-foot runways compared to the 7,000 to 10,000 feet required by conventional jets. A tilt-wing VTOL, intended for commercial use, is designed with wing and engine units that rotate at right angles to the fuselage, acting essentially as a helicopter rotor. Other models have extra jet engines directed downward. Like a helicopter, VTOL aircraft require no runway space at all.

The development of STOL and VTOL technology would effectively distribute the problem of aircraft noise, for they are planned for an airport system in which the large, long-distance jets would continue to use a central airport but the short-range intercity aircraft would be dispersed to satellite airports. However, prospects for extensive use of STOL in the near future are not promising. The airline industry predicts consumer problems: STOL flights tend to be unstable because they cruise at low altitudes. And a search for STOL site in the New York area suggests that despite the limited airport space required, suitable land is not easily available near congested urban areas, and suburban communities are not likely to welcome airports even if noise is reduced to the level of highway traffic.

Changing Airline Operations

Another way to reduce the impact of noise is to increase the distance between the source of noise and those affected by it. This might involve relocating airports to less-inhabited areas or changing operating procedures. A pilot can make glide-slope adjustments that permit aircraft to approach runways at higher altitudes and make steeper descents. Similarly, on take-off, a pilot can climb at full thrust and then cut back on power over populated areas, resuming his climb at a greater distance from the city. Airport neighbors favor such changes in operating procedures, particularly since concern about noise is often mixed with fear of low-flying planes. Shifts in procedures would not only limit noise but would physically move the air traffic away from the affected community. But the Airline Pilots Association is concerned about safety: "You have to pull power back to the point where you are about falling out of the sky."[21]

Other possibilities include using a preferential runway system, modifying flight paths or displacing the threshold (the point of touchdown) on particular runways. These options are opposed by both airlines and airport operators. Restricted runway use is in direct conflict with efforts to enlarge airport capacity and threatens to decrease efficiency and increase delays. The delay of a plane in landing is estimated to cost $6.50 per minute (this includes fuel, engine wear and flight personnel salaries) and, in addition, there is the cost of time to the passengers.[22]

Perhaps the most controversial noise-abatement proposal to date has been the night curfew. From the community's point of view this is highly desirable, and curfews exist in more than 25 European airports including Paris, Frankfurt, Amsterdam and London. But curfews are strongly opposed by United States airport operators and the FAA, which claims that they would severely disrupt passenger service and air-cargo operations because about half the air freight shipped in the United States is moved between 11 P.M. and 7 A.M. One United States commercial airport, National Airport in Washington, D.C., run by the FAA, has imposed a curfew following complaints from residents—some of them influential congressmen. When the manager of Los Angeles Airport, besieged by billions of dollars in damage suits, suggested a night curfew as a means to relieve his problems, he was strongly criticized by colleagues in the Airport Operators Council: "We cannot afford to let ourselves be picked off one by one in this country. It is already happening in Europe."[23] Instead, Los Angeles imposed restrictions on nighttime flights requiring landings and take-offs to be over the Pacific Ocean. When a state court in New Jersey authorized a small general aviation airport in Morristown to restrict night aircraft operations, the National Business Aircraft Association, the Air Transport Association, 12 airline companies and the FAA intervened.[24] Although Morristown handled only four jet operations per day, such a restriction would have set a legal precedent undermining federal authority to regulate airport operations. As in the case involving Burbank, California, the U.S. Supreme Court ruled against the right of a municipality to restrict the amount of noise allowed from night flights over a populated area.

Land-Use Restrictions

From the perspective of both airlines and airport operators, the most effective noise-abatement policy involves
land-use restrictions that would leave a wide, clear zone in
noise-afflicted areas. Federal guidelines outline categories
of acceptable land use on the basis of the NEF calculations
described previously (see Table 4). The FAA uses these
guidelines to recommend that airports receiving federal aid
be located in areas where use is restricted accordingly.
This, however, is not required as a condition for receiving
federal funds. Fifty-one of the airports serving the 61
largest cities in the United States were built prior to 1950,
that is, well before the introduction of jet service. Since
they were located with no consideration of noise impact
on surrounding communities, FAA recommendations for
compatible land use cannot be fully implemented. This
was recognized by a 1965 Supreme Court decision concerning airport zoning ordinances in Gary, Indiana, which
declared a requirement for compatible land use unconstitutional.[25] Thus, the FAA merely pressures airport authorities to use local influence to prevent non-compatible
institutions (such as schools and hospitals) from being
built in their areas. HUD has also exerted pressure for
compatible land-use planning by setting noise limits on the
location and construction specifications of federally financed homes and buildings.[26]
Airport operators and the airlines want federal legislation to set land-use policy, establish noise ceilings and issue
standards for approach and climb-out procedures that
would affect all airports equally. Airport operators are
especially concerned with land-use policy because it affects
their legal liability. However, antinoise groups are reluctant
to accept a land-use policy that enforces a concept of
"unacceptability" defined by the government or an airport
operator. They seek their own definitions and reject the
language of federal guidelines. One noise-abatement acti-

vist, Robert Baron, denigrates community noise studies as efforts to maintain the status quo by discovering how much noise people will tolerate. Compatible land use, he claims, is "a euphemism for resolving the noise problem by eliminating those who complain about it."[2][7] Furthermore, noise standards that prevent the construction of low-cost housing are opposed by many community groups, which argue that housing is badly needed and should be funded.

Private citizens have brought suits against airport operators in state and federal courts based on two legal grounds: "nuisance" and "taking." Nuisance is based on the principle that each person should make reasonable use of his property so as not to injure another; taking assumes that a public body should not destroy the value of land without compensation. In 1946, the case of *United States* v. *Causby* set an important precedent when the court ruled that use of overhead air space by military aircraft was a "taking." The flights over Causby's farm caused 150 chickens to become frightened and kill themselves by flying into the walls, and the court required compensation because invasion of the air space "affect[ed] the use of the surface of the land itself."[2][8] Although Congress has identified certain areas as navigable air space, some courts have still held proprietors of commercial airports liable for damage to neighboring communities. In an important decision (*Griggs* v. *Allegheny County*) the Supreme Court specifically placed responsibility for the effects of aircraft noise on the airport operator and required the operator to compensate the property owner for damages resulting from aircraft flights. The fact that approach patterns were within navigable air space did not prevent the decision that there was a "taking" of private property requiring compensation by the airport operator.[2][9] Based on this decision, 49 families near Los Angeles International Airport were recently awarded $365,700 in damages to compensate for noise.

Such rulings have left airport operators vulnerable.

However, the law has generally dragged well behind technological changes and the whole new set of problems these changes have created. Most current legal remedies were developed during less complex times; damage awards are usually based on precedents established in the era of propellor aircraft. In most states litigants can recover for damage caused by the invasion of air space directly over their property, but not for the considerable disruption that can be caused by modern jetcraft operations nearby though not directly overhead. A further difficulty is that compensation requires judgments concerning the extent of physical invasion and disruption, factors which have proved difficult to define to the satisfaction of all parties concerned. The prerequisites that nuisance impair the use and enjoyment of a plaintiff's property and that the use of airport property be "unreasonable" are ambiguous and can prove insurmountable barriers to recovery.[30] In addition, plaintiffs often lose their suits because "they come to the nuisance," i.e., the airport was there first. Finally, even if a homeowner is compensated, continued discomfort or the necessity of moving may be personally disruptive to an extent that is regarded as socially unacceptable, as it was in the case of East Boston.

Part II:
LOGAN AIRPORT
AND ITS NEIGHBORS

3

LOGAN INTERNATIONAL AIRPORT

You're one in ten million. Welcome to Boston from the world's eighth busiest airport.
                              —Logan Airport billboard

AIRPORT HISTORY

Logan International Airport emerged out of Boston Harbor, 2,250 acres created by a series of extraordinary land-fill projects. Located only two miles from downtown Boston, the airport forms the point of a densely populated residential peninsula. The city of Boston managed the airport until 1948, when pressure to expand and modernize the facility led the state government to assume control.

In 1945 Governor Maurice Tobin addressed the Massachusetts General Court (the state legislature) on the subject of Logan Airport. He told them that if Boston were "to keep pace with progress" it would need a modern air transportation facility. This, he claimed, required control by a public authority "whose sole responsibility is to bring the project to a speedy conclusion."[1] Several years later in

TABLE 6
Logan International Airport Growth
(1960-1972)

	1960	1963	1966	1969	1971	1972
Scheduled Airline Operations	114,070	122,668	161,675	229,610	242,802	248,076
Passengers*	2,932,231	3,837,124	5,968,948	9,168,936	9,338,764	9,980,325
Cargo (tons)	28,718	44,195	81,454	131,002	131,128	144,743
Logan Employees†	5,500	6,000	7,000	9,800	10,000	10,000**

Source: Massport, Annual Reports, passim.

* These figures include total passengers using the airport and are arrived at by doubling the number of passenger enplanements.

† Not including Massport staff employees or construction workers.

**Estimated

1948, the state legislature established the State Airport Management Board. The city gave the state title to the airport and to Amerena Park, an adjacent waterfront area located in a section of East Boston called Jeffries Point. Legislation at this time also provided for a transaction that was to affect all future planning: the Boston City Council voted to allow the city to give to the state a 70-acre park in East Boston called Wood Island (or World War II Memorial Park) in exchange for East Boston stadium property and Orient Heights (Constitution) Beach. Implemented on August 2, 1954, this exchange developed into a major symbolic issue, setting the tone of all subsequent relations between the airport and its immediate neighbors.

The governor and the legislature directly controlled the State Management Board during the years between 1948 and 1959, and its financial support came from taxes. The next five years saw corruption and bad management. By the mid-1950s the airport, caught in the vicissitudes of Massachusetts politics, was a burden on the legislature. It had accumulated a debt of over $42 million, which cost Massachusetts $3 million annually in principal and interest payments.

In an effort to relieve the tax burden and to remove airport development from the pressures of special political interests, the legislature passed the Massachusetts Port Authority Enabling Act in 1956 to set up a "public instrumentality not subject to the supervision or regulation of the department of public works or of any department, commission, board, bureau, or agency of the commonwealth. . . ."[2] Its responsibility extended to Logan Airport, the Boston seaport, Hanscom Field and, by a later amendment, the Tobin (Mystic River) Bridge. During the next three years the state issued $72 million in municipal bonds to support the airport, and in 1959 the Massachusetts Port Authority (Massport) began its reign.

In 1960, Logan Airport consisted of four runways, two

parallel strips running northeast to southwest (4L-22R and 4R-22L), a single runway northwest to southeast (15R-33L) and another east to west (9-27).[3] The system handled 195,000 operations and enplaned 1.4 million passengers per year. The one long barrackslike terminal building had positions for 45 aircraft. Ten years later, with over 4.5 million passenger enplanements and 242,800 scheduled airline operations annually, Logan had grown to be the eighth busiest airport in the world[4] (see Tables 6 and 7). Massport had extended runway 15R-33L by 2,200 feet and expanded landing areas, taxiways, parking and terminal facilities. Existing runways were modified to allow instrument landings; during the spring and summer of 1967 instrument operations increased 40 percent over the same period during the previous year.

Massport based its expansion program on its projections of future demand. It expected passenger travel to grow at 7.6 percent a year through 1975 and 5.3 percent annually thereafter; 8.3 million enplaned passengers were anticipated by 1980. Air cargo, used regularly by about 4,000

TABLE 7
Airport Facilities Summary
Boston-Logan International Airport
(1972)

City/County	Boston/Suffolk
Ownership	Mass. Port Authority
Total Acres	2,250 (approx.)
Scheduled Airline Service	19 Certificated Air Carriers
	11 Commuter Airlines
Hangars	8
Runways	
4L-22R	7,850 ft.
4R-22L	10,002 ft.
9-27	7,002 ft.
15L-33R	2,468 ft.
15R-33L	10,090 ft.
18-36 (STOL)	1,800 ft.

New England businesses, was predicted to increase to
184,000 tons by 1980.

TABLE 8
Forecasts of Airport Operations at Logan Airport
(Total Operations*)

	1975	1980*	1985
Forecast made in			
1970 and 1971	388,400	455,700	511,500
Forecast made			
in 1973	317,100	359,100	393,000

Source: Preliminary environmental impact report, "Extension of Runways 4L
and 9 and Construction of STOL/GA Runway 15-33," Landrum & Brown,
December 1972, p. 20.

*Including military and general aviation.

Projections of future demand on an airport vary, depending on the significance the forecaster places on past
growth rates, general economic trends and anticipated
economic and legislative constraints on growth. Table 8
presents 1971 and 1973 forecasts of future Logan Airport
operations as estimated by Landrum and Brown, a consultant firm hired by Massport. When both passenger enplanements and aircraft operations decreased during 1970,
Massport consultants interpreted this as an anomaly. Projections that included data on the 1970 decline were
exactly the same as projections made earlier on the basis of
1969 business. Yet, during this same period American
Airlines was predicting a zero growth rate as the basis of its
own planning decisions.[5] Only later, when traffic declined
from 316,744 total flights in 1971 to 301,609 in 1972, did
Landrum and Brown revise its forecasts.

Based on demand estimates, the big expansion thrust at
Logan Airport began in 1967 with plans for a new runway
parallel to 15R-33L, extensions of runways 9 and 4 and
for the development of the Bird Island Flats area to the
south of the airport for air-cargo facilities, hangars and a

new STOL runway.[6] By mid-1970 airport plans included
four separate terminals with positions for 90 aircraft and
parking for 8,800 automobiles.[7]

Profiting by the "jet boom" of the 1960s the airport has
become a large, financially sound institution. Its stark,
spacious, modern architecture is striking in its densely
populated urban setting full of old triple-decker wood-
frame homes. The contrast is symbolic and important in
understanding the intensity of community opposition. The
airport is a sort of city within a city; a subculture of
mobile, middle-class citizens who thrive on the conve-
niences of a facility that is devastating to a community
that shares few of its benefits. That is not to denigrate the
airport's economic contribution to Boston. It employs
about 10,000 people and uses an average of 1,750 construction workers each year. Its operations contribute
several hundred million dollars annually to the Boston
economy in direct expenditures (wages, construction and
maintenance costs and purchases).[8] However, its jets release some 84,000 pounds of contaminants each day,[9] and
the negative impact of noise affects some 100,000 people
in East Boston, Revere and Winthrop.

THE PUBLIC AUTHORITY

Public authorities develop from adversity and the recognition that other forms of government are unable to
cope with problems. As soon as things get tough,
authorities will be created. If the airport is controlled
the burden will fall on the taxpayers. There will be rapid
deterioration of the economy, employment, and the tax
base.
                        —Massport Director of Aviation[10]

Massport is a perfect example of the violence and

tyranny of an institution. In our country we are always talking about democracy. An institution can become so powerful that it is a violent institution.... They are becoming a power unto themselves, and I think it is high time we control them; because if we don't I can think of one city that's going to go right down to oblivion.
—Community Representative[1][1]

Massport is one of at least 18,000 public authorities in the United States.[1][2] Set up by city, state or national governments as autonomous, special-purpose bureaucracies, these authorities are financed by tax-exempt revenue bonds. Their function has been to get specific jobs accomplished efficiently with minimum drain on public monies.

Often called "special municipal corporations," public authorities proliferated in the 1920s and again in the 1950s with the increase in large public construction projects. Their marginal position between the private and public sector has enormous advantages. As government bureaucracies, public authorities own tax-exempt properties, are free to establish monopolies and are immune from regulation by other state agencies. They also have powers of eminent domain and access to public credit. Yet they enjoy the advantages of private enterprise. Being free from state supervision and independent of the legislative appropriations process, they need not be responsive to political issues. Furthermore, they are exempt from civil-service regulation and other conditions of state government employment; they are generally able to pay higher wages than regular government agencies. Given such advantages in an expanding market, many public authorities have been successful in serving the narrow functions for which they were established. Yet the fragmentation of governmental functions into autonomous bureaucracies creates its own problems.

Financing projects through tax-exempt revenue bonds places fiscal control in the hands of people unaffected by the projects they support. This method of financing raises serious problems of public accountability; public authorities must give the highest priority to meeting their obligations to bondholders, and as a result they tend to maintain a limited perspective, focusing on specialized and narrowly defined objectives. And they may ignore local demands that involve broadening this perspective, especially if these demands pose a threat of financial uncertainty or risk. Despite their formal insulation from the political process, public authorities are necessarily political because of the scope of their decisions. While they may not be attached to traditional party alignments, they tend to be caught up in the political differences of class-based interest groups. In fact, until recently appointments to public authority boards have long been based on political obligations. Like western European ambassadorships, they were generally given to prominent men as part-time prestigious favors. As public authority activities have become controversial, appointments have tended to be more representative. For, as Robert Smith argues, along with the authorities' interest in efficiency must be a concern for the electorate. "Efficiency is but one desiderate of a governing unit; another is the sensitivity to public will."[1][3]

The Massachusetts General Court saw several advantages in creating a public authority to manage Logan Airport. Totally financed by revenue bonds and user charges, it would relieve the tax burden of the previous arrangement and facilitate the heavy capital investments required for airport expansion. Massport could run its business free from the uncertainties of legislative appropriations and from the pressures of a political scene colorfully described by a reporter as "poisoned politics. . . . The political processes of Massachusetts are deeply infected . . . jobs, contracts, and miscellaneous favors have become the life-blood of Massachusetts politics . . . a nightmarish world of vendetta and intrigue."[14]

As intended, the combination of financial and political autonomy gave Massport flexibility to meet the objectives of efficient and rapid growth. Since 1959, Massport has spent or committed about $350 million on development and improvement projects. Its expenditures have been financed partly by income from operations including the tolls from the Tobin (Mystic River) Bridge but mainly by large bond issues.[15] And despite the local significance of its decisions, Massport is accountable primarily to these bondholders.[16]

As for Massport's relation to political demands, the governor of Massachusetts has no direct means to control Massport's activities. He has some indirect influence on policy through his power to appoint the seven members of Massport's board, but once appointments are made he has no authority to bring the board's actions in line with state priorities. Massport's financial and legal autonomy limits political intervention. And, with its control over jobs, over contracts for a high-cost, expanding facility and over numerous tax-free concessions, it has a great deal of potential leverage in the legislature to further its own priorities.

Unquestionably, the dominant figure in Massport's organization is Edward King, its executive director. King was the comptroller and accountant when Massport was established in 1959. He soon became secretary-treasurer, and in 1963 the board named him executive director. At 46 years old King has the highest paid job in state government, $54,000 a year in 1972. (The state secretary of transportation and construction earns $35,000.) King is a very controversial figure—regarded as competent, energetic and effective by some, callous, insensitive and inflexible by others. He runs a highly centralized and efficient business and is personally involved in every decision, ranging from

major construction projects to small contracts for daily
maintenance. He is reputed to patrol the airport personally, seven days a week. Proud of his accomplishments at
Logan Airport, King has little tolerance for opposition. A
quotation from a speech by Winston Churchill is framed
on the wall over the reception desk in Massport's front
office:

> Never give in,
> Never, never, never, never
> Never yield to force and
> the apparently overwhelming
> might of the enemy.
> Never yield in any way
> great or small, large or petty
> except to convictions of
> honor and good sense.
>
> —speech at Harrow, 1941

King sees around him self-seeking political activity and
feels that airport opponents are only a small minority of
"rabble rousers." He believes that his plans to expand the
airport are rational and necessary; if Massport does not
expand, increasing air traffic will saturate the existing
facilities and cause danger and inconvenience. Since the
world is not a utopia, King claims, it is inevitable that the
airport which benefits many people causes problems for
some. He notes that Massport serves nearly 10 million
passengers annually. Four thousand New England businessmen use the airport for commerical shipping. "By far the
greatest good for the greatest number has been realized."[1][7]

Massport has an administrative and legal staff that holds
some of the best paid jobs in the state (see Table 9). They
implement policy that must be formally approved by a
majority of the seven board members, each serving two-

TABLE 9
Salaries of Public Officials (1972)

Position	Massport	Mass. Bay Transit Authority	Mass. Turnpike Authority	Department Public Works	City Government
Top Administrative position	$54,500	$40,000	$41,376	$28,856	$40,000
Job Title	Executive Director	General Manager	Chairman	Commissioner	Mayor
Secretary/Treasurer (or Controller)	$37,980	$29,918	$30,535	$16,442	
Highest paid division director or department head	36,503	33,656	26,060	22,664	30,000
Chief counsel	31,650	33,660	26,060	17,219	25,000
Chief engineer	30,000	22,510	27,645	22,193	

TABLE 10
Massport Board Members, 1959–1973

Name	Date of First Appointment	Primary Occupation
O. Kelley Anderson	1959	Insurance Executive, New England Mutual Life Insurance
Ephraim A. Brest	1959	Lawyer, Financial Consultant
William B. Carolan	1959	Banker
Carl J. Gilbert	1959	Business Executive: Chairman of Executive Committee, Gillette Co.
Nicholas P. Morrissey	1959	Labor: International Brotherhood of Teamsters
John S. Pfeil	1959	Sr. Partner of Stone & Webster Engineering Firm
Philip H. Theopold	1959	Business Executive: Director First and Second Fiduciary Fund
Hirsch M. Swig	1961	Real Estate Developer
Laurence O. Albre, Jr.	1962	Business Executive: President, Albre Tile Associates

Thomas G. Brown, Jr.	1963	Banker: Vice President, State Street Bank & Trust Company
Charles A. Connors, Jr.	1963	Business Executive: President, Hub Linen Supply Company
Edward C. Maher*	1963	Banker: President, Home Federal Savings & Loan Association of Worcester
Howard W. Fitzpatrick	1964	High Sheriff, Middlesex County
Anthony D. DeFalco*	1969	Business Executive: Director, Franchi Construction Co., Special Assistant to U.S. Secretary of Transportation
Frank J. Harrington, Jr.*	1969	Business Consultant
John L. Thompson*	1969	Lawyer; President, Massachusetts Blue Shield
Albert Sallese*	1970	Reverend: East Boston
William F. Lyden*	1972	Labor: International Brotherhood of Teamsters
James A. Fay*	1972	Professor: Engineering, MIT

*Board members as of May 1973. In July 1973 the governor appointed Michael Wood Christian, an attorney, to replace John Thompson.

year terms. The special commission that proposed this structure to the General Court in 1956 sought as members of the board "distinguished community representatives who represented no particular interest groups and who could be counted upon to lend their prestige in a representation of the multiple interests of the greater metropolitan community."[18] When the General Court created Massport it drafted an Enabling Act stipulating that the board include people with experience in engineering, finance and commerce, plus one representative from a labor organization. To ensure neutrality, it required that the party affiliations of board members be balanced, with no more than four members belonging to one political party. Such a structure was founded on several interesting assumptions: that the governor could find neutral or representative individuals to serve on the board; that controlling party affiliation was a meaningful way to balance existing interests in the Commonwealth; that these interests were definable and predictable over a seven-year term; that professional business leaders plus one labor leader constitute a complete set of possible "community" representatives.

Since it was first established in 1959 the board has had 20 members, mostly from the legal, business and banking professions (except for the labor representative as required by the Enabling Act; see Table 10). Until April 1970 when Reverend Albert Sallese, a clergyman from East Boston, was appointed to represent community interests, this group shared a point of view compatible with that of the executive director. There was little dissension; board members, unpaid and with full-time and demanding occupations of their own, served essentially as a rubber stamp for staff recommendations. Only the staff itself has had the time, the interest and the access to expertise required for making the basic policy decisions.

The board's operating procedures suggest its limited authority. Board members meet monthly both in executive session and in an open meeting lasting three to five hours. During the open meeting they handle business concerning

TABLE 11
Agenda for a Massport Board Meeting
September 21, 1972

Off-Shore Oil Study

Extension of Runways 4 and 9 and Construction of STOL Runway

Design Proposal

Noise Barriers—Jeffries Point

Inventory Control System—Mystic Terminal

Laser System for Monitoring Ships in the Approach to Runway 4R

Expansion of Mystic Container Terminal Berth

Logan Airport Duty-Free Shop

Rent-A-Car Agreement

Passenger Handling Charges—Non-Scheduled Carriers

Consolidation of Schiavone Operation at Mystic Pier

First Street Track

Recommendation for Awards for MPA Contracts: Reconstruction of Approach Light System Runway 4R; Boiler Replacement, Hoosac Pier No. 1; Demolition of Portion of Shed 2, Castle Island Terminal.

MPA Contract No. 1.113—International Terminal Roadways and Car Parking Areas, Change Order

Reconstruction of North Apron Taxiway and Adjacent Hangar and Cargo Aprons

Route C-1 Ramp Modification Study—Neptune Road Vicinity

Executive Director Report on Proposed Third Tunnel, Governor Sargent's Proposed Plan for Acquisition of Boston & Maine Railroad Corporation, and Status of Sea-Land, Inc.

Demetri Enterprises, Inc.

BU Building, Maverick Street, East Boston

Marriott Corporation—In-Flight Meal Kitchen

Airport Master Plan

Source: From Massport, Board of Directors Meeting, *Minutes*, September 21, 1972

the seaport, Hanscom Field and the Tobin Bridge as well as
the airport. Airport business ranges from decisions about
specific contracts and agreements to the most general
discussion of long-range plans. An agenda from one meeting suggests the variety and complexity of decisions that
are made within a few hours (see Table 11).

Board meetings are held in a small conference room at
the Massport city office. The executive director, the
secretary of the board and Massport's general counsel sit
around a long table with the seven board members. Five
rows of bridge chairs are set up for the press and observers.
Since December 1971 the proceedings have been recorded
and the minutes transcribed. When board members enter
the meeting room they receive a folder listing and describing the day's agenda. Only in rare instances is written
material distributed prior to the meetings.

Each issue is introduced by King or a staff member who
describes the problem and presents staff recommendations.
The board itself seldom raises policy issues, usually dealing
only with staff suggestions. In some cases the board will
create a subcommittee to look into a specific issue, but by
and large the meetings are ad hoc and decisions are made
with relatively little information. The staff, by contrast,
has prepared and digested the material and comes to the
meeting prepared with a motion to be voted on following a
brief discussion.   Discussions became increasingly conten-
tious when Albert Sallese was appointed to the board in
1970 and began to present the point of view of those
opposed o Massport expansion. Only when these new
issues were raised ' did the implications of Massport's
independence from the political system become fully
apparent. It was soon clear that Massport's mandate, its
financial obligations and above all its internal structure
allowed the organization to resist influences that could
significantly broaden its special-purpose orientation and
temper its principle of continued expansion.

4

"EAST BOSTON IS NOT AN AIRPORT"

East Boston is not an airport; it is the closest thing to one.

—poster in East Boston Little City Hall

THE NEIGHBORS

In the nineteenth century, East Boston was known as the Noddle Islands, the home of McKay shipyards and their famous clipper ships. East Boston harbor was the hub of the East India trade and New England's growing international commercial interests. It reached its peak as a residential area in 1925 with a population of 64,000. Today it is a working-class, residential community, containing 37,404 people primarily of Italian origin.[1] More than one-fifth of these people are over 60 years old. Most are Catholics, and the many churches and parochial schools are an active and important part of community life. The population is relatively stable and homogeneous; the wood-frame, multifamily, "triple-decker" flats of East

63

Boston have housed the same families for many years. One-third of these families earns less than $6,000 per year. About 1,000 people in East Boston work at Logan Airport, primarily in low-paying jobs. According to Massport's own data in 1970 the average annual wage paid by Massport to East Boston employees was only $4,344.

The West End and other Italian neighborhoods in Boston were destroyed by urban renewal; East Boston was spared. But the Boston city administration had for the most part neglected the area, assuming that it would inevitably decline as the airport expanded. While city neglect kept out bulldozers and left neighborhoods relatively intact, East Boston's real undoing was transportation. Since 1934, state transportation programs have cost the community over 1,000 units of housing and 70 acres of recreational space taken from three neighborhood parks. The access roads for the Sumner and Callahan tunnels that connect East Boston with downtown took 170 properties. In 1951, the expansion of the MBTA line and, four years later, a new state highway split the community, cutting off a major residential area, Neptune Road. The airport itself occupies two-thirds of the total land area of East Boston.

Herbert Gans described Italians in Boston's West End as "urban villagers" with many characteristics carried over from southern Italy. These include an intense mistrust of government bureaucracy, which they see as "engaged in a never ending conspiracy to deprive the citizens of what is morally theirs."[2] As redevelopment programs broke up the West End in the 1950s the "villagers," fatalistic about their capacity to influence the outside world, remained politically apathetic. East Boston has many of the characteristics of an urban village as described by Gans. Like the old West End it is divided into tiny neighborhoods; if one asks an East Bostonian where he is from, he will name an area defined in terms of a local street, school or parish.

Normally, he will respond actively only to issues that directly affect his own area, for this is the only place where he has a sense of influence. East Bostonians also tend to be suspicious of outsiders, especially if they are from the government or large bureaucracies. They are convinced that Massport is conspiring to drive them out and pessimistic about the possibility of influencing bureaucratic decisions.

However, unlike the West Enders, "Easties" have expressed their mistrust by becoming highly politicized. According to one community organizer, "Everyone is a leader in East Boston and no one is a follower." Each neighborhood has its own favored political leaders. Elections for public office draw many candidates and a large voter turnout; 44 percent of the total East Boston population came out to vote in the 1972 state Democratic primary. The excruciating experiences of redevelopment in other parts of the city awakened East Boston to the consequences of apathy, and when an urban renewal group came to the community in 1969 to explain an intended project they were forcibly driven out.

Primarily, it was the history of transportation disruption that politicized East Boston. John Vitagliano, present manager of East Boston's Little City Hall,[3] drew up a list of 40 transportation issues that have become controversial in the community over the years; 23 were airport-related problems (see Table 12). In East Boston, the airport stood for middle-class convenience as well as oppressive bureaucracy. These associations converged with discomfort from noise and pollution to create intense resentment. The visibility of the target, and sufficient external support to suggest the possibility of success, provided the motivation for political action. As one resident noted, "We are obviously at war with the Massachusetts Port Authority and other insensitive authorities and big business officials who have, by their actions, deeds and maneuvers, almost destroyed and continue to attempt to destroy what is left of our lifestyle and of the physical boundaries of our residential community, which has only a thousand acres left."[4]

TABLE 12
Airport-Related Problems in East Boston

Loss of one thousand units of housing (1934, 1951, 1961, 1967)
Air rights over community (1934 to present)
Loss of 70 acres of recreation space (1967-68)
Loss of access to Boston Harbor due to land fill programs (1947)
Deterioration of schools and playgrounds from noise (1947 to present)
Trucking on Neptune Road (1967)
Block-busting tactics (1960 to present)
Massport attempt to acquire East Boston Stadium (1966)
Massport attempt to acquire air rights for garage (1966)
Scare tactics concerning land acquisition at Jeffries Point (1966)
Massport attempts to chase the independent cabs out of Logan (1964)
Expansion into residential districts (1967)
Expansion of runways into Wood Island Park (1967)
Proposed new runway affecting air and ground traffic (1969)
Low-flying aircraft (1967 to present)
Air pollution from aircraft exhaust and from trucks (1947 to present)
Affect of land fill on harbor (1970)
Use of Tobin Bridge tolls to pay Massport lobbyists in legislature
The inequities of tax-exempt status of businessmen on Logan property
Trucks traveling over speed limits to deliver land fill (1970)
MPA opposition to elderly housing project near Maverick Square
MPA opposition to waterfront park in Jeffries Point
Lack of "real" master plan

Source: John Vitagliano, Manager of Little City Hall

AIRPORT IMPACT

Homes, schools, streets, churches are exposed to extreme danger from low-flying planes as well as high levels of noise and air pollution. In fact, a TV antenna on Neptune Road has been knocked off by the tires of an airplane.[5]

—East Boston resident

East Boston's concern with Logan Airport began in 1945 when the state government authorized the Department of Public Works to spend $15 million to expand the airport land area. Opposition in the state legislature failed to block the airport expansion bill, but a recreation plan was also developed and financed by the state as, in the words of Mayor James Curley, "a small compensation for

TABLE 13
Noise Impact of Logan Airport

| | Within NEF 30 | | Within NEF 40 | |
	1967	1975	1967	1975*
Acres of land affected	16,200	52,000	3,630	7,010
Number of people affected (September 1970 revision)	177,000	556,000	29,500	55,200
	(94,000)	(340,000)	(18,000)	(43,100)
Number of schools affected	93	272	7	33
Number of pupils	44,500	155,500	4,000	15,700
Number of hospitals	6	12	1	2
Number of beds	1,391	3,158	560	625

Source: Peter Franken et al., *Aircraft Noise and Aircraft Neighbors*, Bolt, Beranek and Newman, Cambridge, March 1970.

*Calculated without SST.

the burden the people of East Boston are carrying toward development of an airport they never sought."[6]

Logan Airport affects East Boston in many ways. The jet blast from planes flying over homes on Neptune Road, a section of East Boston directly on an approach to a major runway (15R-33L), has not only knocked down television antennae but stripped the leaves of trees. Signals from instrument landing systems obstruct television reception. A church steeple and its bells had to be removed as hazards to low-flying aircraft. Oil pipelines to the airport have raised homeowners' insurance rates. Federal standards on compatible land use have prevented needed housing construction and, with a history of residential disruption due to highway and transit development, the housing issue is a highly sensitive one in East Boston. But the primary impact of the airport is noise, mainly from aircraft but also from airport construction trucks and service vehicles that move through city streets.

In 1970 a consulting firm, Bolt, Beranek and Newman, contracted with DOT and HUD to analyze the noise

TABLE 14
Attitudes Toward the Aircraft Industry
in Boston

	True	False	Undecided
Aircraft designers doing all they can	54.97	27.53	17.50
Airport operated in best interest of city	56.52	35.25	8.23
Airport authorities doing all they can to eliminate noise	39.19	42.80	18.01
Airport authorities not very much concerned with average citizen	51.03	42.97	6.00
Airline companies will do nothing unless forced	67.67	24.36	7.98

Source: TRACOR, "Community Reaction to Airport Noise," NASA contract NASW 1549, September 1970.

impact of Logan Airport operations. Using the NEF contour system described in chapter 2, the study documented the noise impact in 1967 and estimated the noise contours for 1975 based on Massport growth projections (see Table 13). According to federal guidelines, values of NEF 30 are incompatible with schools and hospitals and exposure to NEF 40 is incompatible with all residential land use.[7] Not surprisingly, the Bolt, Beranek and Newman findings were welcomed neither by Massport nor by the federal sponsors of the research who tried to prevent their circulation. The City of Boston filed suit on February 26, 1970, under the Freedom of Information Act, and DOT released the report on March 17, the day before scheduled court hearings.

Another study appeared in 1970; it compared public awareness of airport noise in seven United States cities, including Boston.[8] In it, 1,166 persons within 12 miles of Logan Airport were interviewed. Of the seven cities, Boston had the highest rate of negative attitudes toward aircraft operations and the second highest rate of complaints. 46.5 percent of the Boston sample reported sleeping difficulties due to aircraft noise; 34.3 percent feared the planes were flying too low for safety. Yet in mean noise exposure Boston rated fourth among the cities in the study. One finding suggests a possible reason for the high rate of complaints; more than half of those interviewed in Boston had a negative image of the airline industry and airport operations (see Table 14).

The intense feeling provoked by noise, fear of accidents and frustration with Massport's planning procedures are dramatically expressed by East Bostonians themselves.[9]

"Noise Makes People Irritable"

I have 2 children at high school, they say noise is so

unbearable teachers have to stop talking at their classes. It happens all day.

Back yards are not of much use when they are noisy. Noise makes people irritable and it is impossible to carry on a conversation with a neighbor making for isolation of people.

They used to have concerts at Marine Park in the summertime, they were just a waste of money. You couldn't hear the music with the noise of airplanes.

We shout to be heard until we get hoarse and then we just stop communicating.

It's impossible to talk on the phone, or listen to the radio, or watch television without being interrupted by the noise of the planes.

Sometimes we just bury our heads in the pillow. Have to hold our hands over our ears the noise is so terrible.

My hearing is partially gone. My wife is a nervous wreck, the children are high-strung from tension.

If we took pills for nervousness we would be taking them all the time.

We all have headaches, nervousness, are irritable from constant noise.

"I Thought a Plane Had Struck the House"

Several people in the community, especially small children, are extremely frightened by airplane noise.

Babies are awakened during the day and at night. This also frightens the parents, fearing the child may be ill.

I manage a Little League baseball team. I can see the fright in a boy's eyes and actions when planes are landing and he's at bat. Also the High School conditions are deplorable.

When a plane flew very low in January 1970, the reverberations were such that a 60-pound antique mirror hanging on a two inch spike rode down the wall about an inch before shattering to fragments. Needless to say, I thought a plane had struck the house and almost wound up in the street wearing pajamas.

We live in constant fear of airplane accidents due to very low-flying planes directly over our house.

How would you like to look up from your yard and wonder if a plane is going to clear your roof?

I have actually had company leave my home because the planes were flying so low, they were petrified. They told me, if you want to get together again, please visit us, because as long as those planes fly that low we will not visit you.

Some nights I get about 3-4 hours sleep. I go to work very nervous from fright and lack of sleep.

"Hitting Against a Stone Wall"

In making complaints you get the feeling that you are hitting against a *stone wall*. Everyone is very polite and soothing, just be calm and the noise will go away.

Apparently no one, with the exception of Mr. King, has any authority to answer anything. For about a year now I have given up calling hoping to spare myself aggravation added to what I already have. The soothing manner of the professional public relations type doesn't soothe me.

I have complained repeatedly since the week after we moved here and realized that the noise was worse than at our previous home. I joined the Massachusetts Anti Pollution & Noise Abatement Committee, League of Women Voters, made countless phone calls to [Massport], City, Federal and State Officials, written letters and telegrams. The noise has not abated.

Those planes that warm up at 2 and 3 A.M. and then take off is unnecessary in my judgment. I honestly think a lot of it is put on just to make people miserable.

We all agree an airport is necessary but they have become an authority higher than our government, with absolutely no regard for our right to privacy and tranquility. All we ask is the right as Americans to live as our neighbors, who I'm sure don't want a second airport in their back yard. The time has come when the rights of people come first. Only then can we win back the respect of our children; and only then can the State Government win back the respect of the people.

One must live in East Boston to genuinely gather the utter frustration that is felt when dealing with an insensitive authority that we did not create and which we cannot control.[10]

Massport's response is mixed. On the one hand, the staff has argued that the noise *is* in places intolerable and that compatible land-use policy would suggest that these areas, in particular Neptune Road, be evacuated. On the other hand, there is a strong feeling among staff members that complainers are "trouble makers" or "rabble rousers" and that many complaints are gratuitous and related to personal problems as much as to objective conditions. A Massport consultant observes that:

> Noise is an increasing problem everywhere in urban life and how one reacts is highly dependent on his attitude and how much "pre-conditioning" was present. We are sure that few industries have given so much attention to reducing noise levels as has the air transport industry.[11]

COPING AND COMMUNITY ORGANIZATION

> I have considered moving many times to avoid the noise but my husband is retired and his friends and family are all in this area. Also our rent here is less expensive and we can't afford to pay more.

Some people have left East Boston; some have tried to leave but cannot afford the move; others think about moving but their roots are deep and they are reluctant to make the change.

Why don't more East Bostonians simply move away? In a study of an Italian working-class community in another section of Boston, Mark Fried and Peggy Gleicher have described the localism characteristic of working-class communities and the sense of belonging and commitment to a residential neighborhood. People are committed both to local social relationships and to physical places. Commitment extends clearly beyond the dwelling unit to a neighborhood that becomes highly important as a source of satisfaction and personal identity. The neighborhood is an "integral part of home," providing "the core of social organization and integration."[1][2] The profound consequences of dislocation for the lifestyle of such groups helps to explain the intensity of the response in East Boston and the willingness of so many residents to put up with noise and discomfort even when given the opportunity to move.

Those who remain cope in various ways; staying away from home as much as possible or seeking means to make home life more bearable by soundproofing, air-conditioning or planting trees as a sound barrier. But many people feel uncertain about the future of their homes and neighborhoods and they are reluctant to invest in expensive repairs or improvement, anticipating further airport expansion that will reduce property values if not take their land. "Why don't you tear down all of East Boston, South Boston, Winthrop and turn it all over to the Airport?" asked one resident. "Then you could have real long runways. All the way to Dover and the other suburbs, saving commuting time for the travellers."

East Boston citizens are knowledgeable about the details of airport operations and engine types that affect the noise level. And they have definite ideas as to how Massport might change its operations to reduce their problems. Most of their proposed solutions involve changing Massport operating procedures: consolidating flights, curfews, high-altitude landing and preferential runway use. Some people propose that Massport soundproof East Boston homes. Others hope that a second airport will be built to relieve the area or resort to fantasies:

One day the people of East Boston took Logan Airport by eminent domain. 34,000 people slept through the night in a terminal; and the next day they made runway 4-22 into a go-cart track. Wood Island Park was replanted, and East Terminal was turned into an airport museum. Ed King, the former director of Massport, responded "I think you'll see an eventual resolution of this situation. No, I would not say this is a real setback." He moved to the state house and given a job as chief resident Sanitary Engineer.[13]

The airport has been the predominant political issue in East Boston and the basis for organization and activism in a normally divided community. In October 1972 the six candidates for a seat in the state legislature disagreed on issues such as busing and low-cost housing, but they all stated that their first priority was to stop airport expansion and to gain some community control over Massport decisions.[14] George DiLorenzo, who had helped organize the first East Boston demonstration (see chapter 5) and was one of 12 people arrested for driving through a state-police barricade during an antiairport demonstration in 1969, won by 164 votes. He promised his constituents to get rid of "outside forces like the Port Authority" and to return control to the people of East Boston.[15] Other politicians such as State Senator Mario Umana also regard the airport as East Boston's primary problem, "Everything else is secondary including drugs, schools, transportation, and recreation . . . . There are certain Massport agents trying to tear this town down."[16]

Most political activity takes place through the many East Boston clubs and agencies. A list of community organizations put out by Little City Hall includes four employment-training centers, five recreation programs, 33 community and service organizations (excluding health-related groups) and four voluntary community advisory committees—on drugs, on health, on police and on land use, planning and recreation. Many of these organizations are "airport watchers," for whatever their primary activity they often find themselves confronting Massport. For example, the neighborhood council's effort to buy land for a home for the elderly was obstructed because Massport wanted to keep the site undeveloped. Through these organizations, community leaders take issue with almost every Massport decision regardless of how innocuous it first appears to be. They mistrust the authority ("We find a fishhook in every good-looking piece of bait.") and fear that its every move will lead to further encroachment on their land as Massport seeks to expand its operations.

A major exception to the pattern of active airport opposition are East Boston's many sports clubs. Massport's director, Edward King, a former Baltimore Colt, gives about $100,000 a year to these clubs, and Massport has built a lighted little-league field on airport property. Sports club directors are in a vulnerable and uncomfortable position; they need money and facilities to run sports activities that are desired by the community. But, at the same time, their acceptance of Massport funds is viewed by antiairport groups as "a sellout" that threatens the long-term future of the community. Many sports club directors publicly support Massport and seek to undermine the efforts of airport opponents by questioning whether they are really representative of the community.

One of the most active antiairport organizations is the Neighborhood Council. Since 1968, this group has sub-mitted 200 bills to the state legislature asking for a five-year master plan for the airport to be approved by East Boston prior to implementation, community approval prior to land purchasing, noise controls, curfews and compensation for damages caused by noise. Most of the bills were feasible, but clearly some were politically unrealistic, such as a bill to change the structure of the Massport board to include five community representatives. East Boston's power in the legislature is limited. The spaghetti dinners that East Boston groups can provide are weak competition against Massport's sophisticated lobby-ing. The only bill proposed by East Boston that was enacted into law was one that prohibited Massport from collecting bridge tolls from vehicles bearing the remains of deceased veterans.

A redistricting plan proposed in February 1973 further weakened the community's legislative influence. To maintain its two representatives in the state legislature, East Boston requires a population of 46,462. This is 9,000 more than the 1973 census estimates. The redistricting committee resolved the problem by putting Jeffries Point and Bayswater with a Winthrop district, and part of Eagle Hill with Charlestown. A considerable part of the anti-airport activity has come from these areas, which are all directly affected by airport noise. Separating them from East Boston was viewed as a means to weaken effective political action concerning airport issues in the legislature. DiLorenzo, whose constituency is from Jeffries Point, called the decision "a new airport power play" and accused the redistricting committee of collusion with Massport.

In addition to proposing legislation, community representatives try to negotiate directly with Massport, with the FAA and with city and state government representatives. But their greatest source of influence has been the ability to mobilize hundreds of people for public hearings or demonstrations that dramatize the problems of East Boston and draw support from "outsiders" who share their interest in controlling the activities of Massport, if not the intensity of their feelings:

> They spew their fumes and vomit gasses,
> They torture eardrums of the masses.
> Children cringe and old folks sigh
> When the monsters of the sky
> swoop like vultures claiming prey,
> All through the night, all through the day.
> Oh yes! to leave would be the answer

to rid ourselves of Massport cancer,
But fight we will, and fight we must,
now it's only God we trust.[17]

—Eleanor K. Welch

5

PLANS
AND PROTESTS

Massport began its airport expansion program in 1963 with a plan to extend a runway toward Wood Island Park and the residential area on Neptune Road. Initially, few people took notice of Massport's plan, but by the time it was implemented in 1969 it had been challenged by lawsuits and public demonstrations involving hundreds of East Boston citizens. The "taking" of Wood Island Park assumed an enormous significance in the Logan Airport controversy. It was the first of many controversial actions and set the tone of East Boston's response to Massport's subsequent proposals.

EARLY EXPANSION PROJECTS[1]

In 1963, Massport applied for FAA funds to clear Wood Island Park and purchase East Boston property along Neptune Road in order to extend runway 15-33. East Boston's first antiairport group, the Logan Civic League, immediately responded. The Civic League won a significant victory in May 1963, persuading the state legislature to pass a bill prohibiting Massport from taking, by eminent domain, land west of the airport except in an FAA-required "clear zone." Massport ignored the legislation and moved to acquire land for the runway extension. This required taking three buildings on Neptune Road that housed eight families. In 1964, the Massachusetts Supreme Judicial Court permitted this acquisition as an exception to the legislation, calling Neptune Road "an enclave of the airport." A Neptune Road resident sued, and a bitter series of state and federal court battles postponed construction of the airport extension for five years.

Meanwhile, two jets skidded into Boston Harbor in 1965, increasing the pressure on Massport to expand the runway system. Community spokesmen, hoping to save the homes and Wood Island Park, asked that the proposed new runway be extended toward the sea, and East Boston Senator Mario Umana and Representative Ralph Siriani introduced several bills in the state legislature to prevent the acquisition of Neptune Road. But Massport claimed there was no alternative to extending the runway, and in August 1966 the State House of Representatives supported the plan. A reporter from the Boston *Herald* assessed public sentiment. "The desire of one small community cannot be allowed to stand in the way of progress, particularly since noise problems are rapidly being solved in other ways."[2]

Massport promptly sought legislation to authorize the change in the harbor line that was necessary to build the runway. Then, the Boston City Council entered the debate, opposing airport expansion on the grounds that Massport should pay taxes to compensate for increased annoyance to citizens. But, in early December 1966, the FAA announced that if the extension of 15-33 were not approved it would reallocate the $2 million of federal funds to other states. Massachusetts Governor John Volpe addressed a special session of the legislature strongly urging approval of the Harbor Line Bill by emphasizing the importance of federal funds for airport expansion to the industrial development of Massachusetts. He made one concession to East Boston, "the only obstacle to the passage of this legislation." He promised to see that Massport would fulfill its promise to "replace the recreation facilities of World War II (Wood Island) Memorial Park."[3] On December 28, 1966 the Harbor Line Bill became law, authorizing the construction of the 2,127-foot extension of 15-33 into Wood Island Park. Four months later, in April 1967, FAA funds for the expansion were received and in one day Wood Island Park was graded to the level of the existing runway.

To Massport's staff, Wood Island Park was a "rundown dangerous place." "When I visited that park I felt I was risking my life." But to East Boston residents the park was an attractive and important family recreation area:

> To my recollection, Wood Island Park was lots of trees and grass and a great beach. It was like a green jewel. There was no reason to go away in the summer . . . . Sunday afternoon at Wood Island was the way of life . . . . How many Sunday morning football games were played in the grass field? Who can remember the old bathhouse perched on the hill . . . . What was old Chipping Bridge and where was it? And who knows where Dizzy Bridge is? Wood Island was also a great place for love.[4]

For many people, the taking of the park was "the Alamo." Unable to block Massport with traditional tactics of legislative appeals the Logan Civic League lost its influence in the community; its most active members formed the East Boston Neighborhood Council to develop a more forceful strategy of opposition.

As a final step in getting authorization for the runway extension, Massport sought approval from the City of Boston Public Improvement Commission (PIC) to close 700 feet of Neptune Road. During PIC public hearings in July and August of 1968 alignments began to form. Massport had the support of the federal and state governments and the airlines; the Neighborhood Council was backed by city government.[5]

Massport claimed it needed to take part of Neptune Road in order to meet federal requirements for a clear zone and a "localizer," an instrument to guide aircraft approaches. Mayor Kevin H. White hired two consultants to challenge Massport's claims.[6] In the fall of 1967 they submitted a report concluding that federal regulations could be satisfied without disrupting Neptune Road: the localizer could be placed on airport property, and it would be possible to displace the threshold for aircraft landings over this area of East Boston enough to meet the clear-zone requirement. During this technical debate, the five-year-old case concerning Massport's right to take residential property on Neptune Road reached the United States Supreme Court; it refused to review the case, thus upholding the ruling of the lower courts. On October 15, 1968, the very day after this decision, Massport evicted the eight families on Neptune Road and razed their homes.

Several months later, the Public Improvement Commission decided to abide by the advice of city consultants and refused to approve Massport's request to take 700 feet of Neptune Road. Massport replied that its enabling act provided the legal basis to take by eminent domain "any property deemed by it essential for the construction and for the operation of any project." Barriers were placed around the property and eminent domain proceedings began in February. As a last effort to save the area Fred Salvucci, the mayor's consultant on transportation, met in Washington, D.C., with Chester Bowers, the director of the

FAA, to explain the importance of Neptune Road to East Boston and to present specific technical suggestions on ways to avoid taking the land while at the same time maintaining safety margins. Bowers agreed to explore alternatives, but former Governor Volpe, who had just been appointed United States Secretary of Transportation, took the initiative and asserted, "Through the FAA I am now responsible for hub air safety. This necessitates the closure of Neptune Road."[7] Early in the morning of April 23, 1969, 35 men cut down the 35 elm trees on Neptune Road and evacuated the neighborhood.

Until the eviction of the Neptune Road families, East Boston activists had tried to influence Massport primarily through letters, complaints, lawsuits and appeals to state and federal legislators. However, 1969 became a year of demonstrations: sit downs, slowdowns, stall-ins and blockades. New organizations formed, old ones became politicized.

This new form of protest began in Jeffries Point with the Maverick Street "baby-carriage blockade" of September 1968.[8] Over 600 trucks used Maverick Street each day on their way to and from the airport. The city had asked Massport to build a road on airport property for the trucks but King had refused. Residents suspected that Massport had long-range plans to take all of Jeffries Point and that using city streets as a truck route was an attempt to harrass them into selling their property. On September 28, a group of women and children parked themselves on Maverick Street, physically blocking Massport trucks for a week. This demonstration was well publicized and brought wide attention to the East Boston dilemma, certainly more attention than the losing battle on Neptune Road. Boston police were called in but proved sympathetic to the demonstrators. Later, Mayor White ordered the police to turn back the trucks while he and Governor Volpe negotiated with Massport. The city's earlier request was met; Massport agreed to construct a new road on airport property parallel to Maverick Street but separated from the neighborhood by a hedge.

The incident had considerable impact on East Boston. The success of the Maverick Street women and children reinforced a growing sentiment among airport activists: "Legally we couldn't get anywhere. The only way we could get anywhere was to demonstrate. If you write a letter, they put it on a desk and there it sits."[9] Success led to an increase in the number of people in East Boston who were willing actively to oppose airport expansion. Indeed, a few months later East Bostonians joined a city-wide demonstration against highways, carrying "stop airport expansion" signs. When Francis W. Sargent replaced John Volpe as governor of Massachusetts in January 1969, "Easties" demonstrated at the state house, asking support for 15 bills to curb Massport. And three times during the spring of 1969 East Boston residents blocked or slowed down traffic in the tunnels and on the Tobin Bridge near airport access roads. By showing once more that the community could impede airport operations, they hoped to persuade Governor Sargent to give East Boston a voice in future airport decisions. The traffic slowdowns were well organized; residents in various neighborhoods were linked by a system of "telephone trees" for instant phone communications. During the third demonstration, members of the Greater Boston Committee on the Transportation Crisis (GBC) and students and residents from other areas joined the East Bostonians. Massport obtained a court order and used state police assigned to the airport to break up the crowd. However, the demonstrations slowed traffic for several hours, causing flight delays and, more important, they once again directed a great deal of public attention to the East Boston dilemma.

Incidents during the following summer focused on Maverick Street and the Jeffries Point area. In the spring of 1969 the East Boston Neighborhood Council appointed a committee to discuss the possibility of reclaiming Amerena

Field, which had been given up by the city in the original transfer of the airport to the state in 1949. Massport had authorized the construction of a post office and mail facility on Amerena Field, which is located near the site of the Maverick Street demonstrations. The community fought this plan, engaging the support of U.S. Senators Edward Kennedy and Edward Brooke, but Massport refused to relocate the facility, agreeing only to build fencing and to plant shrubbery between the post office and the residential area.[10]

The demonstrations against airport expansion were taking place during the "jet boom," a period of increasing demand for airline service. These trends had led to several studies on the possibility of a second airport. A report projecting the air transportation needs of the New England region through 1990 was prepared for the Boston Redevelopment Authority (BRA). Presenting evidence on travel demands, noise pollution and automobile congestion, the BRA indicated that a second airport would be necessary by 1980 and recommended immediate action to acquire and develop a site for a new airport which would handle all long-distance operations. With a second airport, Logan would eventually be restricted to short-haul trips within the Northeast corridor.[11] Based in part on the arguments presented in this report, the BRA opposed further investment in Logan expansion.

Another study was done by a group of MIT engineering students who designed Project Bosporus, an offshore airport outside Boston Harbor.[12] During this time Massport consultants Landrum and Brown, Inc., recommended both expansion of Logan and development of a second carrier airport in Dover, Massachusetts, with a dispersed system of general aviation airports. Finally, in June 1970, an Interagency Committee on the Boston Metropolitan Airport System concluded a study initiated in 1965. The committee unanimously agreed that the Commonwealth of Massachusetts should reserve an appropriate site within eastern Massachusetts for possible use as a second major carrier airport.[13] The majority of the committee thought that the best location would be Hopkinton, but the MAPC in 1969 recommended that the second airport be located in the Uxbridge-Douglas area.[14]

Each participant in the Interagency Committee filed a minority report with site recommendations, and each proposal met a negative response. A convenient airport was desirable, but it seemed that no community wanted one close by. For example, shortly after the Interagency Committee report was released, an organization called Hopkinton Against Land Takeover was formed to oppose the construction of an airport in that area. Another group, the Anti-Airport Executive Committee, composed of 27 community representatives from 13 towns, formed to exert political pressure on the governor to oppose a second airport. There was, apparently, no site within the state where a second airport could be built without opposition. Surveying this situation in 1973, an Arthur D. Little report prepared for the Massachusetts Aeronautics Commission ruled out a second major jetport because of the difficulty of acquiring the necessary 10,000 acres of land. The report recommended instead the development of a small suburban airport to relieve Logan of general aviation and short-haul flights. After this second airport debate, it seemed that the major burden of meeting air-travel demands would be retained by Logan Airport.

NEW EXPANSION PROJECTS

The Second Parallel Runway

The demonstrations of 1969 did not deter Massport's plans. In September 1970 it applied to the Army Corps of Engineers for a permit to fill part of Boston Harbor for a

new 9,200-foot runway parallel to 15-33. With this major
addition to the runway system, Logan's capacity would
increase from 368,000 to 417,000 annual aircraft operations; without the addition, Massport predicted, the airport would reach saturation by 1974. The new runway
would provide all-weather landing capability, and Massport
argued that the increase in flexibility would relieve noise
because it would be possible to divert traffic from runway
22L, which was closer to private homes. They also claimed
that delays would decrease, and these in turn would reduce
operating costs for the airlines.[15] The only environmental
costs of the new runway, according to Massport, would be
the elimination of 93 acres of polluted clam flats and 250
acres of wildlife preserve that constituted a hazard anyway
because birds interfered with the jets.

The Corps of Engineers required a public hearing, and a
remarkable one took place on February 26, 1971. One
thousand people showed up, and for 10 hours politicians,
administrators, engineers, priests, schoolteachers and other
citizens debated over the priorities that they felt should
govern airport decisions. Sixty people delivered prepared
testimony, mostly opposing airport expansion. Massport
staff members were backed by their consultants, the Air
Transport Association, the State Pilots Association and the
Boston Chamber of Commerce.

Massport's staff stated their priorities: to meet passenger
demand for airport growth and to serve the economic
well-being of the region. The consultants provided a brief
environmental statement for the meeting, arguing that the
new runway would have no direct detrimental effects of
ecological significance. Furthermore, because of the added
flexibility, the runway would relieve congestion caused by
the expected increase in aircraft operations. Failure to
expand the airport as proposed would cause delays, increase air pollution, reduce safety margins and have a

"drastic" and "immeasurable" impact on local economy, "an impact which the Boston area could not afford."[16] The testimony of Massport's consultants at the hearing dealt in technical detail with the airport's impact on birds and shellfish. Their focus on fish caused evident frustration among observers, most of whom had come to the hearings to express how the airport had disrupted their personal lives.

Until the plans for this latest expansion were released the neighboring communities of East and South Boston, Winthrop, Revere and Chelsea had not coordinated their opposition to Massport. In August 1970, however, the Jaycees (Junior Chamber of Commerce) from the nearby city of Winthrop formed the Massachusetts Air Pollution and Noise Abatement Committee (MAPNAC). MAPNAC developed from a local Winthrop group to a coalition, including citizen groups from other affected communities, working to convince the governor and the state legislature to impose controls on Massport. Organizations that had been active on the highway issue now broadened their interest to include the airport. John Vitagliano, an engineer and activist later to become manager of East Boston's Little City Hall, became MAPNAC's full-time coordinator.

The Corps of Engineers hearings on the proposed runway were a convenient opportunity for MAPNAC to publicize its demands: that Massport publish a five-year master plan for the airport, set up an airport advisory committee of seven members representing communities affected by noise, restrict the operation of certain aircraft, impose penalties for noise infractions and pay damages to affected areas. MAPNAC helped organize active and influential opposition at the hearings, bringing in many political representatives from local and state government as well as several U.S. senators and congressmen. MAPNAC also involved conservation groups, the League of Women Voters, local planning agencies, community organizations and labor unions as well as citizens from neighborhoods directly affected by the airport (see Table 15).

The issues raised were diverse. Neighborhood people

TABLE 15
Presentations at the Corps of Engineers Hearing
February 26, 1971

Groups Represented	Number of Representatives
Public Officials	
U.S. Congress	5
Governor's Office	1
State Legislature	12
Mayors and Their Aides	4
Councilmen and Selectmen	5
Planning Commissions	2
Massport	
Staff	2
Board members	1
Consultants	3
Industrial Interest Groups	
Aviation	2
Shipping	1
Labor Interests	2
Civic Organizations and Citizen Groups	
Primarily concerned with political or other issues	8
Primarily concerned with environmental issues	10
Community Representatives	
Church affiliated	6
School affiliated	4
Individuals from affected areas	12

spoke of the discomfort and uncertainty caused by aircraft
operations and of Massport's piecemeal and closed decision-making procedures. Environmentalists talked of the
destruction of Boston Harbor and planners related airport
decisions to general urban problems. Finally, 27 politicians
expressed their concern with Massport's autonomy and the
antagonism between administrative bureaucracies and elected officials. Ten hours of public debate revealed general
cynicism and mistrust of unwieldy bureaucracies and
resentment toward experts who seemed to turn complex
questions of values and priorities into simple economic and
technical certainties. According to Congressman Thomas
("Tip") O'Neill, "No consideration has been given to the
ecosystem and to the needs and welfare of the people . . . .
The members of Massport have prostituted themselves to
the pursuit of the almighty dollar to the exclusion of every
consideration."[17]

The hearings ended with issues aired but unresolved;
plans were made to reconvene after Massport completed
the required environmental impact study on the proposed
new runway. This study commissioned to Landrum and
Brown Airport Consultants, Inc., at a cost of $166,000
was released in May 1971.[18] As the airport opponents
predicted, it documented Massport's contention that the
new runway was essential for safety and would be environmentally advantageous; it emphasized the positive contributions of Logan Airport—its economic importance to the
city of Boston, and the reduction of noise that would
follow from increased runway flexibility. Expansion of
Logan was recommended as "the best opportunity to
realize a reduction of current social impact." The report
described and rejected, one by one, the alternatives proposed by airport opponents. Banning specific types of
aircraft "interferes with interstate commerce." Limiting
maximum permissible noise levels is "legally questionable," since the airport functions as part of a coordinated

national system. A surcharge for noisy aircraft would be "useless" as economic leverage, since landing fees represent a negligible percentage of total airline expenses. Setting night curfews is "precluded" by the interdependence of flight schedules and aircraft utilization requirements. It would relegate Boston to a "second-class" airport and have "disastrous effects" on service to 65 percent of the 267 cities served by Boston. Moreover, 70 percent of the cargo business would be "negatively affected." Soundproofing neighboring houses and buildings would be "economically prohibitive" and have little effect. The only feasible solution to noise and environmental problems, according to the Landrum and Brown report, is an adequate and flexible runway system that would permit a preferential runway use program. The consultants assumed that the anticipated increases in demand for airport service would occur whether or not Massport expanded its facilities. Massport's legal responsibility, according to its consultants, was to enlarge facilities to meet such demand; to do otherwise would violate its legal obligation and have negative environmental effects.

The city of Boston rebutted the environmental impact statement in a presentation to the Metropolitan Area Planning Commission (MAPC) on June 24, calling the statement "the logical outcome of efforts directed toward narrow objectives."[19] City representatives contended that Massport's authority to restrict aircraft noise was in fact limited neither by the FAA nor by the enabling act, that the FAA actually encouraged airport operators to restrict airport noise independently. They argued that Massport's assumptions concerning anticipated demand for increased airport capacity were questionable and in any case were subject to modification by consolidating schedules and dispersing general aviation flights. Figures concerning the economic impact of expansion and the consequences of a moratorium on expansion were debunked as "blatant puffery." As for Massport's contention that the new runway would be environmentally advantageous, city representatives concluded that an expanded airfield would only expose new populations to increased noise. Instead, they recommended short-range efforts to increase capacity at Logan through scheduling adjustments and long-range efforts to develop high-speed rail service in order to drain off at least part of the traffic between cities in the Northeast corridor.

These differences were to be aired at a second round of public hearings scheduled for July 10, 1971. However, on July 8, following a task-force study that recommended alternates to expansion, Governor Sargent intervened and publicly opposed the construction of the new runway. For Massport to hold a hearing under these circumstances, with all of the leading elected officials of the state openly opposed to the plan, would have been extremely embarrassing. And the Corps of Engineers was unlikely to approve a project that was specifically opposed by the governor. Thus Massport withdrew the fill permit application and temporarily put aside plans for the project. One and one-half years later, in February 1973, Massport's executive director deleted the proposed runway from the plans for future airport development. Citing projections that were close to those used by airport opponents two years earlier and noting other planned runway extension projects, King claimed that re-evaluation of future needs indicated that a new 15-33 was no longer necessary.

The Outer Taxiway and Bird Island Flats

The new runway was only one of several projects initiated in 1970. In February of that year, the FAA approved Massport's request to build a new "inner" taxiway in a tidelands area of the airport called Bird Island

Flats, near the Jeffries Point area of East Boston. This was
one part of a larger plan to reclaim 200 acres of Boston
Harbor in order to build an area for the growing domestic
air-cargo operations. With FAA approval, Massport began
work in December 1970, contracting for eight million tons
of land fill to develop Bird Island Flats and applying for
$925,000 in federal aid. Then in February, in order to
continue the dual taxiway system around the terminal
complex and facilitate the construction of a proposed new
south terminal, Massport applied for an "outer taxiway"
permit. The FAA allocated $1.1 million for this new
project in May and Massport submitted a final application
for these funds. At this time the authority claimed that
there was no need for an environmental impact study since
there would be no significant environmental effect.

City of Boston planners responded immediately, en-
raged that they had not been consulted about the outer
taxiway—a project that directly interfered with their own
priorities for the area. First, the prospect of eight million
tons of land fill being trucked through city streets was
viewed with alarm. To avoid another Maverick Street
incident, the trucking contract provided that no trucks
would operate after 5 P.M. and that not more than 45
percent of the tonnage would be delivered by truck (the
rest would be delivered by water). This contract requirement, however, proved to be unfeasible. Second, residents
of Jeffries Point opposed a plan that would bring the
taxiway 500 feet closer to their homes and remove a
hangar that served as a sound barrier. They reminded
Massport of its former reluctance to build in areas requiring extensive land fill—doing so might have spared Wood
Island Park. Third, the Boston Redevelopment Authority
claimed the project would interfere with a plan for a
neighborhood waterfront park that had been under discussion since 1965. Massport responded that they had
planned to develop this area since 1956, prior to the city's

acquisition of the adjacent property. The project, Massport claimed, was only one part of a total plan that had been anticipated for years. Any changes reflected needs "dictated by demands of users both as to volume and technology."[20]

Despite growing opposition, Massport awarded a construction contract for the taxiway on June 24, 1971. But two weeks later the FAA returned Massport's application and asked for an environmental impact statement in accordance with the National Environmental Policy Act. Massport complained that the FAA was pressured by the EPA and criticized "the apparent lack of knowledge within the agency pertaining to airport or aircraft operations. It is difficult to understand how a meaningful analysis can be conducted without such knowledge or at least prior consultation with another governmental agency such as FAA who has the necessary expertise."[21]

With construction underway without federal aid, the City of Boston sought an injunction challenging Massport's attempt to bypass federal requirements for an environmental impact statement, claiming that Massport was violating the requirement of NEPA and the Federal Airport and Airway Development Act of 1970 that airport projects must take into account the interests of the community. A federal district court denied the city's motion on grounds that it was not a federal project and that, as such, the court had no jurisdiction in the matter (see chapter 6). A month later the United States Court of Appeals upheld the district court, although it noted that Massport operations were indeed violating the letter and spirit of NEPA.

On February 11, 1972, Massport issued an environmental impact assessment claiming that taxiway noise would have a minimal affect on Jeffries Point compared with normal urban noise, and that the new taxiway would minimize aircraft maneuvering, enhance efficiency and safety and actually reduce peak noise.[22] In fact, failure to undertake the project, Massport argued, would have an adverse environmental impact. Local and federal review of the assessment followed, with DOT issuing its environmental impact statement on July 28, 1972. Final approval was to follow on August 28, at which time Massport would be eligible for federal funds.

However, on August 14 Mayor Kevin H. White, Senator Edward Kennedy and the state representative from East Boston, Monsignor Mimie Pitaro, met in Washington, D.C., with DOT Secretary Volpe to urge him to review the taxiway project in the context of the general situation at Logan Airport. Volpe agreed and, furthermore, promised to withhold further DOT funds for future expansion until Massport developed a detailed master plan. Meanwhile, Massport completed construction of the taxiway and proposed further runway development on Bird Island Flats.

Further Runway Projects

When the proposal for the second major runway parallel to 15-33 was frustrated in 1971, Massport shifted its planning to three new runway projects: an 1,855-foot extension of runway 9, a 2,020-foot extension of 4 and a new 3,830-foot STOL runway, all on Bird Island Flats. The new runways would accommodate an increase in airfield capacity from 303,000 annual flights to 368,000 by 1980. Most of this would occur because of improved air-traffic control equipment, but Massport contended the addition was necessary to avoid airport saturation.

Bird Island Flats had been reclaimed for the new cargo and taxiway development. Still troubled by this development, activists from the Jeffries Point and Bayswater areas adjacent to the flats reacted, fearing that "Bayswater will

become another Neptune Road." A preliminary environmental impact report announced, however, that the improvements would "permit a reduction in overall community noise exposure not possible without these improvements"; in 1980 14 percent fewer people would be in the
NEF 30 area and 8 percent fewer in the NEF 40 area.[23]
(This contention was based partly on the anticipated
future development of microwave landing systems that
would allow a curved approach and the avoidance of
residential areas.)

Massport scheduled public hearings on the new projects
on March 10, but Governor Sargent asked that they be
delayed pending the circulation of a comprehensive master
plan (see chapter 9). His request was backed by written
communications from a congressional delegation including
Senators Edward Brooke and Edward Kennedy, and
United States Representatives Thomas O'Neill, Robert
Drinan, John Moakley and Torbert MacDonald. Meanwhile Massport extended its own invitations to the hearing,
circulating a pamphlet to building-trade unionists: "Please
plan to attend this hearing which could have a significant
impact on construction work and jobs."[24]

On March 1, the Massport board considered the request
to delay the hearings until an adequate overall plan was
available; but, despite congressional pressure, the board
voted to proceed. Hearings were held as scheduled on
March 10. As with earlier hearings, hundreds of people
attended and about 90 registered to speak. Massport
supporters were far better organized than they had ever
been before. Seventeen unionists plus representatives from
local industries spoke in favor of Massport plans as a
necessary solution for Boston unemployment. However,
the governor sustained his initial judgment that it was
impossible to assess the project "except within the context
of an overall plan for the future development of Logan
Airport." He threatened to oppose all federal aid until a

comprehensive master plan was available. Directly challenging this position, in June 1973, the Massport board
voted to undertake an engineering design study for the
controversial runways.

Parking and Terminal Construction

In early 1970, Massport announced plans for the construction of its fourth major terminal building. The design
of the new south terminal was based on a plan for curbside
check-in, including a rooftop garage accommodating 2,700
cars. Close and convenient access to parking was planned
in order to integrate ground and air transportation.

Most people traveling to Logan Airport use private cars.
A Massport travel survey[25] indicates that 84 percent of all
"person trips" are made by private car, 12 percent by
limousine and taxi and 4 percent by mass transit. There are
an estimated 50,000 vehicle trips to and from Logan
Airport each day. In 1971, Logan had a total of 9,281
long-term parking spaces for passengers, visitors and employees plus 425 metered short-term spaces. This was a
surplus of 1,936 parking spaces, but Massport assumed
that the preference for private cars would continue and
predicted a 50 percent increase in parking demand by
1977. Parking is located in or near individual terminal
buildings and in a parking garage, accessible on foot to the
central terminal.[26] Since the older terminals at Logan each
had their own parking, the staff felt it their obligation to
provide spaces for American Airlines, which would occupy
the new south terminal.

The plan for 2,700 new parking spaces brought Massport directly into confrontation with the governor and the
Executive Office of Transportation and Construction. Involved in a $3.5 million review of transportation planning
in the Commonwealth, they regarded traffic generated by

the airport as a part of a larger problem. Airport expansion would generate increased automobile traffic, especially in the two already congested tunnels that connect East Boston and the airport with the rest of the city. Therefore, coordination between city transportation planners and airport planners was necessary for developing a coherent system. Governor Sargent explained his concern at a meeting of the Massport board on December 16, 1971. He argued that increased airport parking would have direct implications for the state roadway system; it would encourage greater use of private automobiles and create the need for a $600 million third tunnel under Boston Harbor. Committed to the preservation of housing and the viability of communities as well as to Massachusetts's economy, the state, as representative of the people, said the governor must "ensure that airport decisions are made within a broad framework of public values . . . . It is not my intention to throttle the airport, it is an efficient and effective airport, but it's got to live in the overall transportation family, and it's got to live in the overall greater Boston community."[27]

Alan Altshuler, secretary of transportation for Massachusetts, claimed that with some adjustment of present facilities a small number of metered spaces would be adequate for five years. Greater convenience of parking would perpetuate the use of private automobiles and increase the already intolerable load on the public highway system. Ultimately this would have an adverse effect on Boston's economy. Altshuler objected to Massport's incremental planning and its assumption that airport decisions were unrelated to the highway issues that concerned state planners. He noted that each specific decision to add parking spaces might seem minor, but if one continuously added spaces as parking demand grew the 20-year increase would be large indeed.[28] If current trends continued, he claimed, by 1977 the existing tunnels would be saturated at peak hours. Altshuler tried to convince the board to consider alternatives such as vehicular "people-movers" from the central garage and the MBTA station, and off-site satellite terminals. "What we are saying is that there are important options which haven't been explored."[29] He requested Massport to authorize a comprehensive study of airport access in coordination with the governor's broader transportation policy, and to prepare two terminal designs for further consideration, one with the garage, the other without.

King responded: there were no practical alternatives. People would continue to bring their cars to airports regardless of increased parking difficulties. To drop parking plans would result in chaos, disorder and inconvenience: "people stopping on roadways, actually parking upon sidewalks, just trying to get rid of their car so that they could get on that airplane."[30] Nothing, King claimed, would be gained by further study; Massport had always done well without outside suggestions.

The board concurred and refused to consider any alternate design but later authorized $9,000 to test the feasibility of a satellite off-airport terminal.[31] The test was to run for 60 days from a single parking area on route 128, and transportation would be provided by Greyline bus at $4.50 each way. King was skeptical from the start, citing a consultants' study predicting that satellite terminals would divert not more than 15 percent of the traffic from airports. Altshuler himself was not appeased by the plans for the satellite experiment. Its high cost and short testing period, he claimed, made it an invalid test of the feasibility of satellite terminals; results were foregone. Moreover, Massport had once again avoided discussion with the State Office of Transportation, treating the experiment as if it were independent of the total transportation problem.

As Massport went on to approve a new bond issue and to award a construction contract for the South Terminal, the City of Boston filed suit charging that Massport had failed to get required approval under state environmental protection regulations. The court ruled that state environmental regulations do not apply to Massport since, in setting up Massport, the legislature had exempted the authority from regulation by any state agency not specifically included in the original enabling act.

The battles go on; old issues remain unresolved as new expansion proposals develop and meet with a similar response. A plan for an oil pipeline system for example is called another arm of the octopus. "It is bad enough that we have oil, air, soil, water, and visual pollution, but now you are even attacking us from underground."[32] New bright flashing runway lights help the safety of Neptune Road but disturb the residents all night long. A containerized shipping facility near Jeffries Point requires more land fill and revives the problem of trucks on city streets. Each new issue reinforces the extraordinary mistrust between East Boston and Massport and brings increasing intervention from city and state government.

Part III:
POLITICAL CONTROLS

6

INTERVENTIONS

CITY GOVERNMENT

Logan airport has been a greedy octopus, threatening
the land and environment of all the surrounding
communities. It is as large as it needs to be. Its mandate
should be to redress the environmental damage of the
past.[1]

—Fred Salvucci

In 1968 Kevin H. White became mayor of Boston,
elected on a promise to focus his attention on formerly
neglected neighborhoods. He began to carry out this
promise by decentralizing City Hall, setting up neighborhood trailers to dispense city services. The first of these
"Little City Halls," in Maverick Square in East Boston,
proved to be East Boston's major source of support in its
opposition to airport expansion. However, Mayor White's
views on the airport reflect more than just his neighborhood policy, for Massport plans have been increasingly
incompatible with other city priorities and responsibilities

as well. Thus, the city law department and various members of the mayor's staff have been involved on a day-to-day basis in the airport controversy.

Massport provides an essential service to many businesses in Boston. Ten thousand people work at Logan Airport at an average annual wage of $9,600.[2] Direct payroll and purchases, estimated at $167 million in 1970, were expected to increase with expansion. But city officials claim that airport services benefit the metropolitan region while costs are borne primarily by the city. The airport ties into the city sewer system, for example, and while Massport maintains its own police force and fire department the city provides supplementary municipal services when needed. Moreover, tax revenues and the tolls paid by commuters crossing the Tobin Bridge help to defray the cost of supporting the airport. Yet airport property and the hotels, concessions and other commercial activities located on that property are tax exempt; in a city of churches, hospitals and universities, Massport owns more tax-exempt land than any single institution. The mayor has tried to introduce legislation that would permit the city to tax hotels and concessions on airport property. Massport, however, fights to maintain the existing system because those businesses that want to locate on airport property are willing to pay higher than average rental rates in lieu of taxes.

City planners also occasionally find themselves in direct competition with Massport. For example, the Boston Redevelopment Authority (BRA) planned to develop a housing project in East Boston that conflicted with a Massport plan for a new container storage area. An East Boston neighborhood park plan competed with the proposed outer taxiway. The city's efforts in East Boston have been obstructed by Massport's reluctance to make available a detailed, long-range master plan. It is in Massport's interest to discourage any development that might in some way interfere with its future projects; efforts to build up East Boston would encourage its residents to have greater concern for maintaining their community, and this could potentially conflict with Massport's interests.

In May 1972 the mayor brought Fred Salvucci to City Hall as his full-time transportation advisor. Salvucci had been manager of East Boston's Little City Hall. He is an MIT graduate with a master's degree in transportation planning, and he speaks both Italian and the technical language of transportation consultants. Totally opposed to aircraft expansion, Salvucci has been, since 1968, an antiairport activist and a link between City Hall and East Boston on political and technical matters relating to the airport.

The city has no authority to exercise direct control over Massport policies. It can only try to influence planning decisions by raising issues in the press, by legislative efforts and by lawsuits. The city spends a great deal of time in court. The law department brings most of its suits to federal courts, hoping that they will take a broader look at the substantive questions involved than state courts, and be less impressed by the fact that Massport is a creation of the state legislature. However, the city has lost all of its cases against Massport. Invariably, the courts have focused on procedural matters and refused to get involved in the substantive social issues. For example, in *Loschi* v. *Massachusetts Port Authority* in 1968, the Massachusetts Supreme Judicial Court upheld Massport's taking of a public way, ruling that Massport's use of eminent domain was within its statutory mandate and that the plaintiff had no standing to protest the condemnation.[3]

Using another tactic in a U.S. district court in September 1970, the city sued Massport for inverse condemnation, arguing that the authority should be required to compensate for damages caused by the impact of jet overflights on 15 East Boston schools.[4] The city based its case on the *Causby* and *Griggs* decisions that airspace is part of the public domain (see chapter 2). Claiming that the direct overflight decreased the use and enjoyment of property, the city asked that Massport exercise its power of condemnation; just compensation would then be required. The court refused to decide the case on the grounds that it lacked jurisdiction to deal with the issues. This decision was based on Massport's role as "an instrumentality of the state." Since Massport was created by the legislature to perform an essential governmental function, the city would have to prove that the action violated state law; defined in this way, this case was also ruled outside the jurisdiction of a federal court.

Then, in 1972, the city sued John A. Volpe, John Shaffer (FAA) and Massport on the proposal for taxiway construction. Again the city failed to convince the federal district court that the issue was a federal question, although it directly concerned compliance with the National Environmental Policy Act.[5] This time the court denied the city's request for an injunction against the Port Authority to halt taxiway construction, arguing as before that the activity was outside federal jurisdiction. And in 1973 the Suffolk Superior Court invoked Massport's status as a creation of the legislature when it ruled that the regulations of the State Department of Public Health do not apply to Massport because the language of the Enabling Act suggested legislative intent to exclude the Authority from such regulations.[6]

In each case the courts have refused to deal with the merits of the issue. In each case, it is assumed that as an agent of the state Massport's actions and their consequences are consistent with "legislative intention." "The legislative history . . . and prior statutes amply show specific legislative awareness of the proposed airport use of the locus."[7] In recent years few courts have refused to judge the merits of a case on such jurisdictional grounds, especially when the problem concerns environmental damage. There is an increasing tendency for courts to come to grips with the substantive issues involved. Some specific cases suggest that the Massport decisions are unusual. In a series of highway location cases, courts have held that projects are subject to federal regulations even prior to DOT authorization for federal funding.[8] And in Boston itself, in February 1973, only six months after the taxiway case, the First Circuit Court backed off from the taxiway decision. In a case involving HUD the court admitted its power to authorize an injunction against actions that frustrated congressional policy and, in particular, NEPA. The court suggested a regulatory scheme that would require applicants for federal aid "to maintain the status quo of the project pending federal environmental review in accordance with NEPA."[9] These regulations would be binding during "pre-commitment" stage, while the environmental impact statement is being prepared. This was precisely the decision that the City of Boston had wanted in the taxiway case. Indeed the court itself questioned its earlier decision. "We confess to a sense of growing uneasiness in seeing decisions determining the obligations of . . . parties under NEPA turn on any one interim step in the development of the partnership between the parties."

The city's aborted lawsuits suggest that Massport's dual power as a public agency and as a private firm gives it an unusual degree of legal protection. If opponents hope to restrain Massport, Fred Salvucci claims, "We will be in court for the rest of our lives." But legal proceedings do delay Massport projects by holding up federal funding. And, in the case of the controversial Bolt, Beranek and Newman report on noise impact, the threat of a city lawsuit forced public circulation of an informative document. In addition, in order to support its legal positions, the city has gathered a great deal of technical information countering Massport's claims, and this has been a source of expertise for community advocates unable to hire their own consultants. Though the city has no direct means to change Massport decisions, its continuing work on airport issues has had considerable indirect influence through its interaction with state government.

STATE GOVERNMENT

I don't think that anyone expects that any administration should take over the day to day control of Logan Airport. What I do want is to have the Port Authority more responsive to the overall transportation problems and to the problems of the neighborhood. I think there should be some means of controlling them . . . . They should recognize that they must be part of the overall greater Boston community.[10]

—Governor Francis W. Sargent

The state government is far more ambivalent about the airport than the city. Massport is formally an instrument of the state. The lines of authority over airport decisions are vague, resting largely on the willingness of board members to carry out the governor's objectives. Massport's autonomy, intrinsic to its structure, only became questionable from the perspective of statewide interests in the early 1970s. Viewing the airport situation in a broad perspective in which regional growth is a major priority, state government officials take a more moderate position than City Hall. Governor Sargent wants decisions that are responsive to local communities, but he also wants to avoid creating local jurisdictions that would tend to fragment a regional transportation problem. As a Republican he has a constituency that includes business and banking institutions and he must be cautious in actions affecting their interests. While City Hall has opposed nearly all airport expansion, the state administration tends to consider separately each Massport project as it relates to overall transportation and economic issues.

Political relationships between state and city government further complicate the airport issue. Mayor White and Governor Sargent were rivals in the 1970 gubernatorial elections, and their relationship has been inevitably influenced by past political competition. The mayor and governor often do agree on particular matters, but their cooperation has been informal, primarily through communication between individual staff members.

The state government virtually ignored the airport debate until 1971. John A. Volpe was governor of Massachusetts until his appointment as United States Secretary of Transportation in January 1969, and East Bostonians remembered him as the governor who "gave away Wood Island Park." When Sargent became governor he immediately faced a major highway crisis. The strength of antihighway opposition in the state had pushed transportation policy from the technical into the political arena and led Sargent to make a dramatic decision on February 11, 1970, to suspend all major highway construction in the greater Boston area. He then appointed, as Massachusetts secretary of transportation and construction, Alan Altshuler, a professor of political science at MIT who had been chairman of the task force that recommended the highway moratorium. With $3.5 million in DOT funds, Altshuler created the Boston Transportation Planning Review (BTPR) to explore alternative solutions to the transportation problem.

Although highways and mass transit were the major concerns of the BTPR, the airport was also a matter of concern to state transportation planners because of the problem of ground access. Surrounded by water on three sides, Logan Airport is dependent primarily on the two tunnels that connect East Boston and the airport to downtown. These have a capacity of 70,000 vehicles per day and are already congested at peak hours (see chapter 5).[11] Governor Sargent, concerned with the increasing demand on the tunnels as well as the growing public opposition to Massport's expansion plans, had to develop a coherent policy with respect to the airport. The old system of transportation planning, in which autonomous agencies worked in technical isolation, was untenable; a balanced transportation system required the cooperation of Massport and other agencies.

In early 1971 the governor appointed the Task Force on Inter-City Transportation, chaired by Robert Behn, to investigate the balance between costs and benefits of airport expansion. Behn was in close touch with Altshuler, having worked with him on the highway study. Altshuler himself participated in the Behn task force and had a major role in drafting the report. Published in April 1971, the Behn report concluded that "the highest priority is to reverse the trend of environmental deterioration in the neighborhoods around airports. Those who benefit directly from air transportation must begin to pay the social and environmental costs of air travel, and specific goals for reducing airport noise should be set before air travel capacity is expanded."[12] The task force agreed with City Hall— that even if Massport's projections were correct existing airport capacity could accommodate considerably more traffic by distributing peak-hour use, improving traffic control and scheduling and establishing landing fees based on runway use. Further expansion at this point, the task force argued, would lead to an increased commitment to air travel at a time when alternate forms of intercity transportation must be considered.

Strongly influenced by this report, the governor developed a new airport policy that began by questioning the technological assumption that "fastest equals best." The costs in noise impact and disruption, he said, must be considered. "What good is technology if it does not better my life, if in fact it may even worsen it?" Reviewing Massport plans in light of the broad transportation goals of New England, he opposed both the new south terminal and the proposed parallel runway. He argued that Massport had not adequately proven its claim that the new runway would reduce noise. "This must be very clear, however, the burden of proof rests with those who *favor* the expansion of the airport not those who oppose it." In addition, he asked Massport to set up a community fund for "pain and suffering compensation" that would be used to sound-proof buildings, provide recreation facilities and develop an equitable policy for property acquisition.[13]

July 8 became East Boston Independence Day, and Little City Hall held an all-day celebration in the stadium. Fred Salvucci called the governor's speech "a grandslam home-run decision." Enthusiasm, however, was tempered by skepticism; "How long will it last?" asked a reporter from the *East Boston Community News*.

The governor's objectives were to integrate Massport's activities with state transportation policy and to press for a planning procedure within Massport similar to that developed by the BTPR. According to this procedure, planners would identify many feasible options for each transportation decision and attempt to assess their social, economic and environmental consequences. These are prepared as "program packages" in which each alternative, including a "no-build" option, is analyzed with respect to cost, service provided and local and regional impact. Then these packages are opened to debate in a series of widely advertised public meetings and workshops. Comments and evaluations are solicited from the broadest possible range of people and institutions concerned with the decision, after which planners revise the "packages" accordingly. The intention throughout is to analyze transportation policy on the basis of both expert advice and public response.

The state transportation policy developed from the BTPR process emphasized public transit and a freeze on all further expressway construction. The single exception was a two-lane special-purpose road and tunnel to Logan Airport, open only to buses, limousines, trucks, emergency vehicles and taxis. Access roads to the tunnel, also limited to common carriers, would connect directly with the Massachusetts Turnpike, the southeast expressway and the proposed south station transportation terminal in downtown Boston. Limiting the roadway system to common carriers would ensure rapid access to the airport.[14] The intention of this plan was to reduce the total number of automobile trips through the existing tunnels by providing efficient and flexible bus and limousine alternatives and, at the same time, to reduce the relative attractiveness of using private automobiles. As a further incentive to attract people to use the service, the governor's plan included a freeze on parking at Logan Airport; instead, four new parking garages and terminals would be built in strategic suburban locations. Massport was asked to finance bus service from these terminals, but state and federal funds would cover the anticipated construction costs of the tunnel (about $200 million) and the terminals (about $20 million).

East Boston activists, supported by antihighway groups, strongly opposed a tunnel—any tunnel at all, "even if you put Italian marble on the walls."[15] From City Hall, Fred Salvucci responded with an informal proposal to once and for all consecrate a no-expansion policy by giving all Massport land outside the runway area to agencies that would develop the land for parks (from which to picnic while watching airplanes) or for natural resource preserves. The assumption was that any improved access would encourage airport expansion.

For quite different reasons, Ed King also opposed the special-purpose tunnel. He argued that passengers would not use public transportation and instead advocated a six-lane, third harbor crossing despite its estimated cost of $600 million. The probable location for the proposed tunnel's portal, given the political opposition from East Boston, was on airport property, and King anticipated disruption of airport facilities. In March, however, the Massport board voted to support the governor's proposal, and King, while still preferring a six-lane general-purpose crossing, agreed to lobby for the proposal. He remained aloof, however, from the BTPR and state transportation planning.

By the end of 1972, the BTPR study was completed. Following its recommendation and also new DOT requirements that urban regions submit unified transportation planning grant applications, the governor developed a reorganization plan that would consolidate many agencies and departments within a centralized transportation department and delegate major related planning responsibilities to locally based regional councils.[16] The regional councils, with representatives from state and local government and private groups, would function according to the participation model established by the BTPR.

The governor sought Massport cooperation in the reorganization and proposed legislation to increase its accountability. However, Massport's cooperation with the governor's transportation plan remains voluntary. Given the financial autonomy of public authorities, Governor Sargent has few direct means to control airport decisions or influence Massport's structure. He does have limited power over some specific short-run projects, since under the Federal Airport and Airway Development Act the state must certify that large airport projects are consistent with state planning priorities before federal funds are allocated. But when no federal funds are involved Sargent has no control over major capital expenditures. There are, however, two indirect means by which he can influence Massport: he can use his power to select members of the Massport board who share his point of view and who are likely to support his policy objectives and he can initiate legislation that would increase Massport's accountability to the state.

Massport Board Appointments

Sargent's first appointments to the Massport board suggested he had no policy with respect to the airport at that time. Frank Harrington was a business consultant who had contributed to Sargent's campaign. Sargent also appointed to the chairmanship John Thompson, a lawyer and member of the Boston finance commission who had also contributed to Sargent's election campaign and who was known to be committed to public service. But as it turned out, he would not constrain airport expansion and sided with Massport's executive director, and against the governor on most controversial issues. Edward Maher, appointed by Volpe when he was governor, was a political activist and campaign contributor to both Republican and Democratic governors, and Anthony DeFalco was a campaign contributor and chief secretary to Governor Volpe.

When a board position opened in April 1970 after the East Boston demonstrations, Governor Sargent agreed to appoint Father Albert Sallese, recommended by the East Boston Neighborhood Council. Father Sallese, minister of the East Boston Holy Redeemer Church, had long been active in airport protest activities. He was a controversial choice, for his former position as chairman of the local Community Action Program (CAP) had exposed him to considerable local criticism. Yet the governor felt he would be the most widely accepted candidate. Later, in 1972, Sargent appointed William Lyden of the Teamster's Union to replace Nicholas Morrisey as the labor representative required by the Enabling Act. Though Lyden's philosophy is broadly in tune with the governor's and the Teamster's Union had backed Sargent in 1970, it is in the interest of his constituency to favor large construction projects.

The appointment of Sallese was Sargent's first effort to broaden representation within the Massport board. Sallese spends nearly half his time on Massport business, investigating all proposals that might affect East Boston. His tactics are to "nitpick"; he continually raises questions that force the board to discuss controversial issues and to delay approval of staff recommendations. As the lone dissenting vote on many issues, at first he had little direct influence on actual decisions, but he gradually helped to make the board sensitive to community concerns. Following his appointment, proposals previously accepted without discussion were approached with considerable caution. Sallese's prodding, for example, helped to create a Massport subcommittee on community assistance, which for a short while seemed to be influencing Massport's attitude toward the problems of East Boston. At Sallese's instigation, several Massport board members visited East Boston for the first time, and several public hearings were held in the community to discuss Massport's policy on home-buying. However, Sallese remained the lone dissenter on most questions until June 1972 when the governor appointed James Fay as chairman of the board; this was Sargent's first major effort to use his power of appointment to bring Massport decisions in line with state policy.

The circumstances of Fay's appointment illustrate the growing tension between Massport and the state government. After his speech about airport expansion on July 8, 1971, the governor negotiated an agreement with John Thompson, who was then chairman of the Massport board, on a 10-point "statement of cooperation" between Massport and State Secretary of Transportation Altshuler.

Thompson later refused to sign the statement, remarking on the difficulty of "two separate government officials perceiving themselves as discharging the same authority and responsibility."[17] Governor Sargent was furious at this rebuff, and in December 1971 he asked Thompson to resign as chairman. Thompson refused and sought support from powerful Boston groups. The president of the Boston Chamber of Commerce voiced distress that Sargent had made the Logan Airport problem a personal issue involving Thompson. A Boston *Globe* editorial criticized "those who would weaken the board by replacing responsible and responsive members with those who would submit to local political control and inevitably cripple the authority."[18] And Raymond C. Rourke, a representative from Lowell in the state legislature and chairman of the joint committee on transportation, accused Alan Altshuler of trying to establish a "dictatorial transportation department" and give his "consulting friends . . . some of the cream at the airport."[19] Sargent's response, according to a *Globe* reporter, "was not publishable in a family newspaper." Following all this supporting publicity, in June 1972 Thompson agreed to step down as chairman and serve the remaining year of his term as a board member.

The selection of a chairman then became an extremely sensitive issue. Edward Maher had been on the board since 1963 and was known to be relatively cooperative on issues concerning community relations. As an experienced board member who had also supported Sargent during the campaign, he fully expected to receive the chairmanship. However, Altshuler had just met James Fay, a professor of engineering at MIT with a long-time interest in environmental problems. Fay had chaired the National Academy of Sciences study group that had investigated the feasibility of a proposal by the Port of New York Authority to expand Kennedy Airport into Jamaica Bay. This group had recommended against expansion and outlined alternative technical and administrative means to relieve airport congestion.[20] Its finding had influenced the Behn task force. In addition, Fay had been chairman of the Boston Air Pollution Control Commission, and he was familiar with Logan Airport problems. He had never been politically active, but his point of view was clearly compatible with that of the Sargent administration, and he seemed a desirable candidate to represent the governor's interests on the Massport board.

Although there was a vacancy on the board, appointing Fay as chairman was politically problematic. Through this appointment the governor hoped to change the balance of power on the board in his favor. Sallese and Maher usually reflected the governor's point of view. DeFalco had been reliable on issues about community relations. But the governor feared that if he selected Fay as chairman, bypassing Maher, he risked losing Maher's support. Just at the time of the decision, Maher showed his ambivalence about the second runway, reinforcing the governor's concern that he could not be counted on. Thus, Fay was made chairman of the board in June 1972.

Maher bitterly resented the decision and was to shift his orientation on many issues that came before the board. In July 1972, at the first meeting chaired by Fay, Maher asserted that "Massachusetts Port Authority is a business organization," and that something had to be done to offset the recent adverse publicity. He moved that the board provide tangible evidence of its support of Executive Director Edward King by granting him a $5,000 pay raise.[21] Sallese objected; he said it would violate the national wage freeze and reminded the board that in Jamuary they had increased King's salary from $48,000 to $49,500, agreeing not to consider another raise for two years. However, other board members were also concerned about the publicity created by the governor's obvious effort to influence Massport. Rumors had circulated that "the transportation czar" (i.e., Altshuler) would next try to oust King. To dispell these rumors the raise was granted and the new board began its tenure with an indication of future alignments.

James Fay was labeled an agent of the governor, and other board members sought excuses to attack him. He was criticized for running up expenses while commuting to Boston from Maine (where he lived while on sabbatical leave from MIT), for causing dissension rather than exercising leadership and for neglecting the day-to-day operations of the Port Authority. Maher has been especially critical. "When John Larkin Thompson was chairman, he spent two or three days a week at the Authority. No one sees Fay. The Authority is not moving ahead . . . there is no leadership under Fay."[22] However, Fay views his job differently from the previous chairman. While he spends less time at the Massport office, he spends a great deal of time coordinating his actions with the mayor's office and with the secretary of transportation, for he feels that one of his major roles is to integrate Massport activities with state and regional planning. As a result, other board members have accused Fay of treating the needs of Massport as secondary to those of the Office of Transportation, of serving as a puppet of the state government. According to Altshuler, however, Fay is far from a puppet. Familiar with the details of substantive issues concerning airport development, his views have had a profound impact on the governor's policy.

Fay's point of view is threatening to Massport. When he attempted to buttress his leadership by requesting that Massport acquire an administrative secretary who would be responsible directly to him, the board objected, fearing that the position (involving access to Massport records) would give Fay too much power. His request was interpreted essentially as a move to take over the authority. Instead, the board created a new post of assistant to the existing secretary-treasurer—who works directly under King.[2][3]

But with Fay involved in the board as well as Sallese, several new and persistent themes began to punctuate the discussions at board meetings. Sallese regarded himself as a representative of "the people" and sought increased public dissemination of information. He also insisted on advance notice of the details of the items to be discussed at meetings: "Put the material in the mail in advance so we have time to read it over," he demanded again and again. Fay, as chairman, hoped the board would take a more aggressive role in determining a policy for Massport, one that would minimize the airport's impact on East Boston and tie its development to the plans of other city and state agencies. To strengthen the board's power within the Massport structure, he asked the staff to present alternative courses of action for the board's consideration rather than simply predigested recommendations. Meanwhile the governor also sought ways to have his appointed board members play a more significant role by asking that they be salaried and spend one full day a week on authority business.[2][4]

Legislation

The governor's office also sought to exercise some direct control over airport noise. Massport has its own noise-abatement committee (LANAC) that is chaired by a Massport staff member and includes experts from airlines, air controllers from the FAA and representatives from the Airline Pilots Association and the Massachusetts Aeronautics Commission. This committee supports federal legislation requiring the airline industry to retrofit their jets, and one Massport staff member is chairman of the environmental committee of the Airport Operators Council

International (AOCI). Their efforts to control noise at Logan have been based on a system of preferential runway use and a policy to develop restricted land-use areas around the airport.

Massport was not in principle opposed to further noise-abatement procedures, and when several board members suggested installing noise-checking stations throughout East Boston they met with no opposition. However, the staff and several board members were extremely concerned about any action that would threaten Massport's autonomy or increase pressure for accountability outside the organization. Thus, they were quite uneasy when the governor proposed the formation of a new noise-abatement policy committee consisting of one member of the Massport board, the secretary of transportation, and the secretary of environmental affairs. Nevertheless, in November 1971 the board approved this committee, authorized it to function on an advisory basis pending the enactment of legislation and selected DeFalco as Massport representative. The board assumed that the governor would submit legislation in 1972 to provide a statutory basis for the committee. DeFalco, Altshuler and Charles Foster (the secretary of environmental affairs) began to work on specifications for a noise-monitoring system and an incentive system that would involve landing fees based on aircraft noise rather than on weight. The committee also made a general review of Logan's noise-abatement procedures.

All went well until January 1972, when Altshuler recommended that the committee's activities be legitimated by state legislation. The bill, submitted to the legislature by Governor Sargent, would have given the committee legal authority to require Massport to follow its recommendations. Federal law, it was argued, recognizes the right of airport proprietors to establish regulations for noise control. Since the Commonwealth created Massport to operate the airport, "it is both necessary and proper that the state legislature . . . should direct them in their proprietory capacity to plan and implement mechanisms for the monitoring and reduction of airport noise."[25] Accordingly, the proposed legislation gave the committee authority to ask Massport to develop noise standards, abatement procedures and monitoring systems. If Massport failed to propose acceptable standards and procedures, the committee could authorize substitute measures consistent with federal regulations. The bill required that all proposals be considered in public hearings and, once approved, they would be binding on Massport.

Altshuler submitted a draft of this proposed legislation to the Massport staff early in January 1972, requesting comment so that details could be worked out prior to the February meeting of the board. He received no response; only at the February meeting did King state the staff objections. The Authority already had a competent noise-abatement staff: "Certainly they are more competent than I am, and I think with all due respect to everyone on the policy committee, even more competent than them, because that is their business. They are air controllers, they are chief pilots, they are noise people with different airlines . . . . You are attempting to supercede another organization on top of an organization."[26] King's concern about losing autonomy was evident. "We could be required to implement something that the Authority didn't vote."[27]

King sought to change the language of the proposed bill, arguing that the noise-policy committee should judge only the "reasonableness" not the "acceptability" of Massport's noise-abatement procedures. Altshuler held the opposite view and thought that if the committee were to have any power to hold Massport accountable it would have to evaluate the "acceptability" of Massport's procedures; judgments of "reasonableness" would leave ultimate authority with Massport itself.[28] He also wanted the proposed legislation to cover all airport-generated noise including noise from peripheral activities such as trucking. However, the board objected and to gain support Altshuler compromised on the scope of the bill and reworded it to give the committee binding authority with respect to standards but not to the means of achieving them. In particular, Altshuler agreed that the tapes produced by a noise-monitoring system would not be used as a basis for legal action. "Any data or information compiled as a result of such systems . . . are inadmissable as evidence and are not a proper basis for an opinion . . . or a matter of which judicial notice may be taken, in any eminent domain or other action or proceeding to recover for injury, damage or a taking."[29]

The final, watered-down version met with considerable criticism from airport opponents; to them it was "that toothless noise-abatement bill." But the board voted to back the legislation and in March asked King to instruct Massport lobbyists to work vigorously for its support in the state legislature. One month later Massport representatives, Mr. William F. Malloy (lobbyist) and Thomas Callaghan (staff member) testified before the legislature's Committee on Natural Resources in opposition to the bill. Other board members were appalled. "Why weren't they up there working vigorously to support this legislation, and if we sit here in an afternoon like we did . . . and went over and around and around on this for two hours, and this is the final outcome of it; shame on us . . . there is something amiss here somewhere."[30] King argued that Malloy's testimony was merely a problem of "emphasis," and in order to rectify the situation, Thompson agreed to write to all members of the state legislature indicating Massport's support of the bill. He sent a letter, but only to the chairman of the Committee on Natural Resources, and the legislature failed to pass the bill. Thus it shared the fate of the hundreds of other legislative bills that had been proposed to control Massport's activities.

The governor's proposed legislation also included a bill to require that Massport seek gubernatorial approval for all capital expenditure projects of more than $1 million, whether or not federal aid was involved. The bill passed the state senate by a 17-16 vote, but the lower house turned it down by a three to one majority.

The governor's failure to intervene through legislation is partly due to the effectiveness of Massport's three well-paid professional lobbyists.[31] The practice of lobbying was developed to enable private interests to advocate their needs to legislative representatives. Its appropriateness as a tool for a public authority is questionable, as it may be argued that a state instrumentality set up to serve the public should have no private interests.[32] Massport staff regards lobbying as absolutely essential to its operations, and from 1969 to 1970 spent more in efforts to influence state legislators than did any other single organization in the state.[33] Some board members clearly are uneasy about the practice. When lobbyist Malloy opposed the noise-abatement bill, Maher criticized the staff for reappointing the lobbyists without board authorization and asked for information about Massport's lobbying activities. "We should not have to resort to the newspapers to find out what our lobbyists are doing."[34]

The governor's efforts to control Massport through legislation was further obstructed by the authority's considerable influence on the legislature. Massport takes care to cooperate with influential legislative interests. For example, as part of its preferential runway use policy, it restricts the use of 4R, Logan's longest runway. The restrictions, preventing all landings, irritate the pilots who feel they need the length for their larger aircraft. But the noise from 4R extends to Hyde Park and several wealthy suburbs that apparently are able to influence Massport policy. In addition, Massport has support from Boston's banking and business interests, a potential source of political contributions to legislators. There are also many favors to be offered in an operation that controls 10,000 jobs, allocates hundreds of contracts and can offer free airplane rides as well. Although originally created to avoid the patronage politics that had subverted the old State Airport Management Board, Massport ironically continues to work effectively in this old Massachusetts patronage tradition in order to maintain its autonomy from outside political control.

7

PLACATIONS

The degree of accommodations and service offered any one segment of the population, however large or small, must be weighed and be in concert with the statutory responsibilities placed on Massport by the Massachusett's legislature . . . Equitable accommodation is not always possible when providing for the frequently conflicting demands of these Massport publics . . . .
—Massport, *Annual Reports*, 1970 and 1971

Since the beginning of antiairport demonstrations in East Boston, Massport has groped for a viable community relations policy. Initially the response took the form of public relations combined with efforts to distinguish the problems caused by airport operations from "needless complaint and harassment." Later, in the face of changes in the board and increasing outside intervention, Massport considered various forms of community assistance and compensation.

PUBLIC RELATIONS

In 1968 the Massachusetts Port Authority changed its name to Massport. The word "authority," was originally intended to imply "authorization," but it also suggested hierarchy and control; it was formally dropped in an effort to neutralize a negative public image. As community pressure continued, Massport emphasized its "good neighbor" activities, citing a grant to a drug-control program, guided tours and courtesy flights, participation in a "help clean up the harbor campaign" and sponsorship of scholarships and educational programs to introduce school children to the transportation industry. One year, Massport ran a school essay contest on "the social importance of the aviation industry." In all, Massport dispenses about $100,000 each year to community-related activities. This is $50,000 less than it spends on advertising directed to promoting Logan Airport as an international gateway and "the fastest airport in the East . . . . the one with no airport stack-ups, traffic congestion or costly travel delays."

Reflecting ex-Baltimore Colt Edward King's personal interest, Massport's major public relations activity within East Boston is support of sports programs and high-school teams. In 1973, $21,700 was budgeted for community sports and athletic awards. Massport also has built (and maintains) a lighted little league field costing $22,000 and a $15,000 playground. A high-school baseball team wears Massport-supplied jackets. The team's symbol used to be the old McKay clipper ship, and the students had worn clipper-ship emblems on their jackets. Now their new jackets, provided by Massport, are adorned with clipper jets; the boys' team is called the East Boston Jets and the girls' team the Massport Jets. The community cannot afford to support its sports clubs alone and needs scholarships. Thus Massport's donations have been important to local youth. In return, recipients either actively support

Massport or at least refuse to join the airport opposition. For example, when the City of Boston sued Massport to compensate for damages to city schools, no teacher in East Boston would testify against Massport and say that noise hampered their teaching. In at least one instance, however, a high-school principal turned down a scholarship offer of $1,250, with a letter stating that there were other matters with respect to Massport's relationship to the community that should be dealt with first.[1]

While attempting to improve community relations, Massport has continued to emphasize its contributions to the Boston economy in general and to East Boston in particular. Following the demonstrations in 1969, wages of local employees began to increase. Even when airline cutbacks reduced the total number of employees from East Boston, increased money in wages went into the community, removing a past discrepancy (see Table 16).

TABLE 16
Wages of Logan Employees

	1968	1969	1970	1971
East Boston				
Logan wages paid to residents	$3,429,434	$3,325,219	$4,343,990	$6,105,170
Number of employees	1,097	985	902	896
Average wage	3,126	3,375	4,815	6,819
Winthrop				
Logan wages paid to residents	3,270,030	3,200,112	3,994,103	4,528,391
Number of employees	662	620	603	590
Average wage	4,939	5,161	6,623	7,675

Source: Massachusetts Port Authority, "Summary of Massport Economy," Massport Public Relations Department Brochure, Boston, 1971.

While increasing wages, Massport warned that restrictions on airport expansion would have dire implications for local employment, as well as for the general economic progress of the region. And a Massport public relations brochure titled "Massport's Needless Controversy," questioned whether the state paid as much heed to evidence of progress as it did to protest. "We sympathize very much with home owners who object to having their lives uprooted to make room for more 747s. But whatever merits their case may have in human terms, similar arguments have never counted for much in the past when progress was at stake."[2]

Massport set up a system to investigate complaints, intending to distinguish justifiable problems from harassment and to provide their own analysis of the impact of noise. This was strongly resented by neighboring communities. Suspicious of Massport's efforts to monitor noise complaints, eight people from South Boston tested the system by phoning in complaints. They then attended the next meeting of the Noise Abatement Committee to find that Massport reported only three complaints from South Boston during the entire preceding month.[3]

In April 1972, when faced with numerous accusations about hearing loss, the board authorized the director of Logan Airport's health service to conduct a study of the hearing of East Boston school children. King was opposed to such a study on the grounds that the public would automatically blame them for all hearing problems that were revealed and that this would invite litigation. The study went ahead despite his opposition, but the board was to receive complaints that King had personally controlled its details, that the sample of children studied was biased with respect to their location in the community and their age and that the results disagreed with other hearing tests: "Funny thing, my son passed the hearing test that was held at the airport recently," claimed a parent. "But he did not pass at Children's Hospital six months ago.

Naturally, I can't help wondering by what standards the children were tested . . . I mean were they tested against a control group of kids from say someplace like Dover or against kids from next to the Los Angeles airport. Of course I shouldn't overlook the fact that perhaps in my son's case, a miracle happened."[4]

Finally, in the summer of 1972, Massport hired a consulting firm to study ways to improve its community image. The consultants reported that the public felt "Massport does not care, cannot be trusted, and seldom acts in the public interest."[5] They made 18 recommendations for both immediate remedial action and a long-term restructuring of community relations. Their report called for delegating authority within the organization so that the board would unequivocally operate as a policy-making body; the function of the executive director and staff would be to implement its decisions. In addition, the report recommended discussion with community advisory committees in order to exchange information about decisions on matters of mutual concern. The consultants predicted that, "If the donnybrook continues, it will lead to a further deterioration of Massport's image despite the Authority's economic and operational success. The eventual result will be diminution if not an almost total loss of confidence in Massport's ability to deal with the public, and an accompanying decline of support by members of the State Legislature."[6]

The board discussed the report in executive session in November and voted not to release it to the public. Two months later, following criticism in the press, they agreed to release it and to establish both a Department of Community Affairs and a Public Affairs Committee. The first would develop and administer projects dealing with community concerns; the second would serve as a formal liaison with those concerned with the impact of Logan operations.

Airport critics regarded Massport's public relations activities as token efforts, attempts to manipulate public sentiment and create dissension within the community. They wanted assistance, but of a sort that would mitigate the problems of noise and community safety and, more important, would compensate for past injustice. In particular, they still remembered Volpe's promise of compensation for the loss of Wood Island Park and felt the airport owed them land. Massport had been able to avoid facing such demands until the summer of 1971, when the opposition in East Boston was reinforced by the governor's new airport policy.

COMMUNITY RELATIONS

Governor Sargent's speech on July 8, 1971, and his subsequent request for Massport cooperation with state transportation planning had included a proposal to compensate communities around Logan for the "pain and suffering of the last decade of accelerated growth." Board Chairman Thompson agreed to create a committee on community assistance and appointed Sallese, DeFalco and Maher, who were sympathetic to the idea of compensation. In November 1971, the committee presented to the board and staff a set of recommendations concerning land-acquisition policy. They asked that the Massport staff prepare a full master plan as a basis for a board review of Massport's land and home-buying policy. This review was to include community participation through public hearings to be held in areas exposed to airport noise.

Massport has taken only four residential buildings through the right of eminent domain but has purchased about 40 homes in the remaining section of Neptune Road and in the Jeffries Point area, often in response to requests by individual residents. Buying homes in response to requests allows Massport to acquire land for future airport development, while resolving some community relations problems by resettling dissatisfied individuals. In June 1971 a Massport consultant interviewed 463 homeowners in aircraft approach zones in East Boston and Winthrop in order to determine whether private homes should be bought. The consultants found that 75 percent of those responding assumed that Massport did not care how much aircraft noise annoyed those who live near the airport; nor did they expect there would be much effort to ease the problem. Since many of these people wanted to sell their homes, the staff regarded their home-buying policy as a community favor.

Antiairport groups, on the other hand, regard this policy as "block-busting." When Massport buys a home, the house is razed, a chain-link fence is built around the lot and a sign is posted indicating that it is now Massport property. This threatens to lower the value of neighboring houses and creates uncertainty so that neighbors hesitate to spend money to maintain their homes.

Following the recommendations of the Committee on Community Assistance, Massport held public hearings in East Boston in January and February 1972 to assess community feelings on the home-buying issue. About 500 people showed up at each of these dramatic meetings and the intensity of community feeling was driven home to board members. Although the focus was supposed to be on home-buying, community leaders used the occasion to express the full scope of their demands concerning airport operation and development. As for a home-buying policy, "We were here before the airport, don't you tell us to move." The community also demanded further public hearings on airport matters.

King described these meetings as uncontrolled, run by "rabble-rousers" who "drove away those who had a right to be there . . . . Decent people who wanted to sell their homes to Massport were intimidated by the rabble. It was crazy. I would not allow my mother to go to a place like that.''[7] King claimed that only six of the 42 people who spoke against Massport's buying homes on Neptune Road were actually from that area. At the next board meeting, however, Maher asserted that "the time has arrived when the public should be involved. We are trying to control a matter of grave concern to a lot of people."[8] DeFalco agreed: "There is no damn doubt that the public feels we are doing nothing to help solve our environmental problems, but are helping to create them. . . . I'm afraid the board has an awesome responsibility."[9]

The hearings convinced the board to vote for a noise-abatement policy committee "that the public would trust," namely one that included members from outside of Massport. And a temporary freeze was placed on Massport's home-buying plans in East Boston. This policy immediately created a dilemma: five families from Neptune Road appeared before the board to plead an exception because of the intolerable conditions in their neighborhood. If Massport was to stop buying homes, they argued, this would not resolve the issue but create greater injustice by blocking all opportunities for people to escape from horrible living conditions. They felt it was the "moral duty" of the port authority to provide relief. King backed their request. "I could not urge you any more plainly or any more strongly than to buy those homes on Neptune Road from the people who want to sell. They are in an area where they really should not be, and when they want to get out and it's in our interest as well to get them out. We have only one choice. . . . I don't want to be responsible for keeping people there who want to move in an area that everyone admits is as noisy as one could expect. It's intolerable living . . . talk about community relations this would be a first step."[10] But DeFalco and Sallese disagreed. Sallese, who had proposed the freeze on home-buying, argued that if the five buildings were purchased and razed by Massport this would make the neighborhood unlivable for others who did want to live there. DeFalco observed, "I sat through every one of those hearings and a 100 percent impression that I got from the communities was that they did not want Massport buying any properties for any reason near those communities."[11] In an effort to resolve the dilemma, several Neptune Road residents formed a committee and polled 58 homeowners in the area; 13 were willing to sell if they received an equitable price, six would consider a relocation plan, five would either sell or relocate if the terms were appropriate and 15 would neither consider selling nor relocating. The rest did not respond at all.

The board could either continue to block Massport's power to buy homes, limiting the rights of those individuals who wanted to leave the area, or it could allow the Authority to buy and tear down homes, thereby threatening other people in the neighborhood. At issue was a conflict between individual rights and the general community effort to stop airport encroachment. James Fay, by now chairman of the board, proposed as a compromise that Massport compensate the five families for the depressed value of their property because of its proximity to the airport.[12] However, a Massport attorney vetoed the proposal claiming that spending funds in this way would violate the bond agreement. In May 1973, Massport dropped its home-buying freeze and agreed to acquire any or all of the 58 dwellings in the noise-impacted area. And later that summer the board voted to buy the homes of 150 families on Neptune Road, to pay up to $5,000 in moving expenses and to buy land for the construction of homes to relocate the community. Initially only 12 homeowners were willing to sell even under such generous terms.

Another community assistance issue was raised in the spring of 1972 when the town of Winthrop requested that Massport pay $160,000 to soundproof a new school. The board was reluctant to venture into "new waters" that would set a precedent for future policy, and Massport counsel again indicated that it would violate the Authority's trust agreement to provide community assistance where there would be no return. The request was turned down. Later, however, in August 1972, the board approved a request to buy Revere school property that was directly on an airport approach on the grounds that it was in the interest of the Authority to minimize the density of people in an approach zone. And again in January 1973, Massport agreed to purchase for $500,000 three old Revere school buildings in an approach zone. This plan aborted, however, when Massport attorneys claimed there could be no assurance on their restricted future use.

As the committee on community assistance continued to seek ways to make life more palatable for airport neighbors, Massport's attorneys took an increasingly important part in policy decisions by interpreting the constraints imposed by Massport's enabling act and trust agreement. Their role became evident in a small but symbolic decision concerning the use of an abandoned building in Jeffries Point, called the BU building. The East Boston Recreation Committee, one of the airport's most tenacious opponents, had requested use of the BU building as a recreation facility for Jeffries Point. Edith D. DeAngelis, chairman of the Recreation Committee, noted that East Boston had half as much recreation space per capita as the rest of the city, and attributed this to "lack of communication, lack of interest, lack of commitment on the part of the city, state, and federal agencies and autonomous authorities which have been gobbling away at our shores as well as our land areas."[13] "The people deserve their birthright," DeAngelis claimed; if Massport would allow Jeffries Point to use the building, this would help repay the old obligation incurred by Volpe in 1966 when he promised that Massport would replace the land acquired through the taking of Wood Island Park.

The Community Assistance Committee recommended that Massport give the building to the community as "an opportunity for the board to ensure the community of its continued existence and that this board will work with the community."[14] King, however, proposed leasing the BU building (valued at $250,000) to Van Dusen Aircraft Supply Company. In 1962, Massport had contracted with Van Dusen and agreed that the company would develop an expanded plant within a new area of the airport near Amerena Park. Subsequently, the state legislature changed the boundaries where taking by eminent domain was permitted, effectively limiting development of this area. Van Dusen brought suit against Massport, claiming a contractual right to expand its facilities. The BU building would help to settle this old dispute and also bring in $540,000 in rent over a 15-year period. Despite King's insistence that there was absolutely no other place at the airport to locate the supply company, on recommendation of the Community Assistance Committee the board agreed to postpone a decision. The committee met with the BRA and Mayor White, and both agreed that the city would develop for recreational use adjacent land already acquired for park purposes. The committee then recommended that Massport work closely with BRA in land-use planning. "We have got to dove-tail on needs because there is just so much land left in this area to meet those needs."[15] As a first step, they proposed leasing the BU building to the city at $1 per year and restoring the Jeffries Point Marina for community use. On their part, the city would have to agree to turn the adjacent property into a community park. This would provide East Boston residents with a large recreation area and, it was hoped, convince them of Massport's credibility and good will.

Both King and Thompson strongly opposed the plan, and 10 representatives of East Boston's athletic clubs came to the April board meeting to claim that the East Boston

recreation committee did not represent their interests. The
decision on the property was deferred from month to
month until, in August, King called in a Massport attorney
who claimed that under the enabling act and the trust
agreement all property negotiations had to be consistent
with the administration of specific airport projects and the
payment of obligations. In his judgment, leasing a property
without an appropriate return would violate the trust
agreement with bondholders, and board members who
voted in violation of this agreement could be sued as
individuals. "Is not better community relations an appropriate return?" asked board member DeFalco. "Were the
trustees interested only in the overall solvency of their
investment?" The attorney took the position that the
existing state of community relations could be interpreted
as "a cost of doing business," and that the trustees were
interested "in each nickel and dime that the authority
collects."[16] As for repaying a past obligation to the
community, "It can't be anything other than a dollar
liability. It isn't a kind of lingering social obligation."[17]

City lawyers disagreed with Massport's legal advice and
offered to formally document the basis of disagreement;
but during a bitter meeting in September the board voted
four to three to lease the property to Van Dusen without
waiting for the city's opinion. No effort was made to
challenge Massport's attorney; it was assumed that his legal
advice was definitive. Two members of the Community
Assistance Committee, Maher and DeFalco, voted against
renting the BU building to the city and the committee was
in effect dissolved.

The issues of community relations raised in the BU case
remain unresolved but the Massport board became increasingly concerned about the eventual implications of its
negative public image. After the consultants report on
public relations, the board began to approve some compensatory measures and voted to establish a new Department

of Community Affairs within Massport. And once more they debated the question of establishing a policy and a set of criteria for dispersing funds for community purposes.

The language of the Enabling Act permits expenditures that are "reasonable and necessary." The test of reasonableness, according to Massport's lawyer, was that expenditures bear a direct relationship to the operation of the airport and be devoted to specific projects approved by the board. The Authority should act "as a good neighbor rather than as a rich uncle."[18] Board Chairman Fay argued that Massport was in fact spending money on community projects that were unreasonable according to the terms defined by the attorney. For example, the current patterns of community support for scholarships and athletic programs failed to pass this "test of reasonableness." Fay pressed the board for a consistent policy. But again the board preferred an incremental approach, for a detailed policy, once articulated, is vulnerable to attack. The community would surely take issue with a policy of "reasonableness" as defined by Massport. Without a policy that would define its future approach to community relations, the board hoped to avoid conflict and to maintain its power of discretion over specific decisions.

Part IV:
AUTHORITY
AND PUBLIC POLICY

8

CHALLENGES
TO AUTHORITY

Noise is a price of progress, a part of our American way of life—argues an airport appraiser. People ought to accommodate themselves. One is reminded of Lord Coke's famous argument in the seventeenth century: "One ought not to have so delicate a nose that he cannot bear the smell of hogs." Yet, Americans *have* largely accommodated themselves to technology and accepted its burdens and bureaucratic imperatives—efficiency, specialization and reliance upon expertise. Objections have been sporadic and individual. Only recently has concern about the negative impacts of technological change been expressed in organized and sustained opposition. Lacking confidence in the ability of the federal regulatory system to implement the necessary constraints, and less willing to quietly move away to less disrupted areas, citizens are increasingly demanding direct participation in planning to assure the protection of their local interests.[1] Many decisions once regarded as prosaic administrative or technical matters have assumed dramatic political content as communities, aware that their local needs conflict with patterns of national development, are asserting their rights as "territories." This activity reflects a number of factors: the visibility of the burdens caused by technological change, the fact that there are fewer places where one escapes these burdens and an increasing confidence that protest will have a reasonable chance of success. The result is community self-protection against new technology that suggests a tendency toward a sort of balkanization or "mini-nationalism."[2] Ironically, it seems that technological changes are fostering the localism and parochialism usually associated with premodern societies.

In order to respond to pressures for efficiency, bureaucracies responsible for technological change are insulated from the uncertainties of the political process, and their inaccessibility is furthered by technical complexity and specialization. At the same time they face counter-pressure—the belief that public officials must be politically responsive to the citizenry. Technological controversies reveal the problems that develop from these conflicting demands for local participation on the one hand and bureaucratic autonomy on the other.

PARTICIPATION

So I say really what is on trial here is not just the Port Authority. It is not just the runway extension. It is really the American system. As we stand here today will it work? Will this board listen to representative government? Will they listen to spokesmen for the people and the people who speak themselves?[3]

—Gerald O'Leary, Councillor

The word "participation" has become part of the popular political vocabulary.[4] Citizen participation is called for in federal legislation. The National Environmental Policy Act and Airport and Airways Development

Act direct agencies to obtain the views of interested groups. The Environmental Protection Agency publishes a brochure called "Don't Leave It All to the Experts" announcing that public participation in decisions affecting the environment is a "must" and urging the formation of citizen organizations. Demands for participation during the 1960s have been recognized in a growing number of public hearings and in increased representation in the membership of the governing boards of corporate and service institutions. Participation in practice, however, is problematic. Public agencies and planning groups set up procedures to include limited participation by those affected by their decisions only to find that such persons conceive of participation in different terms.

Hearings, workshops and other participatory procedures can be used as a way to inform a community about existing plans, to dispel public misconceptions, to permit the expression of public feelings, to reconcile different policy preferences of groups affected by a decision or to expand the range of issues and alternatives considered in the planning process. Even when the intention is to expand choice or to bring new perspectives to bear on a decision, the inclusion of community groups can easily become only a means to gain support for existing plans.

The increased pressure for participation has been disturbing to organizations responsible for efficient technological planning and ironically to community groups when they lack the power to negotiate effectively, given the distribution of resources and expertise. Residents of communities near airports are in a poor position to influence decisions about airport development. Working-class neighborhoods like East Boston are especially vulnerable, but suburban communities find themselves similarly powerless.

Any community opposing a major development faces enormous and complex difficulties, and success often depends on imaginative tactics and a capacity for sheer time-consuming drudgery. It took the success of the baby-carriage blockade on Maverick Street to create an atmosphere in which the East Boston community could organize effectively to oppose airport decisions that essentially ignored the community's existence. Maverick Street and other demonstrations facilitated organization, helping to politicize the community as well as to obstruct airport activities. Even children were affected. A teacher described the attitude of her students. "They were youngsters who had a sense of being pushed into the sea by something they could not control. East Boston is not like that any more. They are beginning to understand that there is power in becoming united, and their town is lifting its head and fighting back."[5]

The tactics used to influence Massport's decisions were varied. Community leaders were persistent, appearing again and again at Massport board meetings, public meetings and demonstrations to articulate community concerns. They dramatized the moral basis of their case, seeking the help of a wide range of parties sympathetic to their cause. Veterans of the antihighway movement and others concerned with general environmental and transportation issues were organized and available. East Boston community leaders also operated at a technical level, using the legal and technical resources of City Hall to develop a competent understanding of airport planning. With this, they hoped to invalidate Massport's position by picking on the inconsistencies in the evidence used to support expansion plans.

In addition, community activists had to bring the discussion to a nontechnical level in order to capture a large base of support within their fragmented community. There was no need to draw local attention to the problem. The impact of the airport on East Boston was tangible, visible and of immediate concern. Enormous trucks hauling land fill, fenced building lots, uncertain property values and above all noise were daily irritants. The most important and memorable single event for East Bostonians had been the taking of Wood Island Park. The destruction of an area that was part of the common experience of the entire community became a symbol of values lost and a focus for political mobilization. References to this event appear in almost every attack on the airport; since the taking many East Bostonians have been convinced that Massport is out to "get" all of its land.

With increased political awareness among East Bostonians, Massport soon became the symbol for a diverse set of problems that troubled the community. At a public hearing a local resident vividly summarized the community attitude toward Massport.

I want to ask ten questions to be put on the record for the Massachusetts Port Authority . . . .

The first question is where does Logan sewage go?

When Wood Island Park was taken away from the people, were they compensated? What did they get out of it? Zap!

Who gave the right to fill in our natural harbor? What political move was there? We have one of the most natural harbors on the east coast, and it is being filled in more and more.

Do the second-class citizens of North Shore who pay the tolls for the tunnels and the bridge, does that money build parking structures, hotels and motels at Logan Airport?

Why does MPA have a tax immunity while the rest of us pay through the nose? They are a sovereign nation sitting out there in itself.

Why do the good dead veterans who gave up their lives for us, why do they have to end up in the baggage compartment? Is this called protocol?

Do the planes have a right to dump waste jet fuel
when they come in? Why don't they dump it on the end
of the runway instead of on our clothes lines and our
homes?

Is the Massachusetts Port Authority a sovereign
nation? Are we a bunch of peasants that surround it? I
work hard all day and walk the straight and narrow, and
pay my taxes, and am very proud of being an American.
I can't even watch a lousy commercial on TV because I
get interruption on the doggone network.

I want to ask the Massachusetts Port Authority one
last question. Are you very happy there?[6]

Massport tended to ignore East Boston demands or to
respond with gestures perceived by the community as
patronizing. Hearings required as a means of public
participation were held and hundreds of people participated, but their influence on policy was limited. The
rhetoric that mobilized East Boston tended to alienate
Massport and also those politicians and administrators
accustomed to a cooler style. Secretary of Transportation
Altshuler, for example, was generally sympathetic to
activists, but observed that "they are so omnipresent,
idealistic, and impassioned in driving home their views,
that it is hard to retain any perspective on the degree of
their wisdom and their representativeness .... I do not
believe that a responsible government can afford to equate
them wholly with the public interest."[7]

The hearings themselves were regarded by Massport
primarily as a way to inform the public of decisions and to
answer any "reasonable inquiries." When the new board
chairman, James Fay, argued that hearings should be a
means to seek opinions from the community *before*
making final plans, he was poorly understood by other
board members.

Fay: I think we should have a meeting with the representatives of that community and explain to them what the proposal is and hear what their criticisms are . . . .

Board member: Did I understand the motion to be that a formal public hearing is to be held? . . . It took us five months to accomplish this?

Board member: Mr. Chairman, if the practice is public hearings on every single thing we are going to do, then we will be having public hearing in regard to the property in Revere, having public hearings on everything we are doing, spending all our time on public hearings. Now, as I understand the position of the Authority, we have a staff that comes in with recommendations to us . . . . I don't see any necessity of us meeting other than with the abuttors. I see no necessity of having a public hearing, irrespective if we were to go there and put in an I don't know what, we are just going to have a lot of problems. Until the plan itself is finalized, I can't see any sense in having a public hearing.

Fay: Presumably the purpose of a public hearing is to get comments so you can finalize the plans, as you say, comments from those who have not so far been heard from.

Board member: Mr. Chairman, I think it would be somewhat unrealistic to expect people at a public hearing to get up and say a new plan for any change by the Port Authority and MBTA is a good idea. We have competent staffs. There is no reason why they can't be charged with the responsibility of informing people so that rumors that are not associated with fact will be dispelled. If it is to be by consensus that the Authority operates, then sure maybe a public hearing will help.[8]

Community members, sensitive to these attitudes, refer to public hearings as a "charade" or a "window dressing for the FAA."

We asked the Port Authority to come down and discuss with us the problems, and about all we got was listened to . . . . The idea is to let the people talk themselves out and that after that they have done that 'we have gotten through another ordeal and we can go along and proceed to fill our airport plans.' "[9]

Thus, in the Logan Airport controversy, public hearings and meetings held to inform the community of plans already crystallized neither established the legitimacy of the planning process nor resolved conflicting preferences, because the issues were already defined and the choices limited. Those opposing airport expansion, unlike many citizens' groups, had some access to expertise through city and state cooperation. They had the formal support of the governor who claimed that "When the actions of the Port Authority have a major impact beyond the boundaries of the airport, and they affect many other interests of the people, then the public must be involved in those decisions."[10] But involvement was difficult; we have seen that the governor himself had limited authority to participate in Massport decisions, and community interests were uncomfortably pressed by relatively limited resources and a time scale determined by the airport operator.[11] In the end, the formal vehicles for participation only aggravated mistrust and further polarized the conflict.

ACCOUNTABILITY

We are closer and more knowledgeable than any other group, no matter what their intentions may be, on what Logan Airport . . . what Metropolitan Boston, what the entire state of Massachusetts and New England needs.[12]
                                                    —Edward King

The Massachusetts Port Authority was created to turn a debt-ridden enterprise into a profitable one, and its effectiveness had always been judged on the basis of the efficient growth of Logan Airport. Given past growth trends and the inherent tendency of bureaucracies to expand, the Authority has been inevitably disposed towards airport growth. Airport development also compensates for the more uncertain economic status of the Boston seaport and ensures Massport the financial stability necessary to maintain continued insulation from legislative influence.

The Authority functions within a system of technological, legal and economic constraints. Its decisions are primarily based on considerations of safety, efficiency, relationships to other air transit facilities, predicted growth in demand, legal requirements and land availability and cost. Many of these considerations are themselves determined by political factors and Massport is continually engaged in negotiation with influential legislators and business interests. Beyond this, however, the complexity of a large-scale facility such as Logan and the financial autonomy of Massport have discouraged public discussion of specific decisions, most of which are judged to be matters of expertise. When social costs are considered in the early stages of decision-making, it is because public resistance is anticipated.

Questions of Expertise

Massport's authority is based as much on its special technical competence in the field of airport management as on its legal mandate. Access to technical expertise is a crucial resource for a public agency. The demand for technology coupled with the deference our society pays to technical knowledge lends a great deal of power to the consulting relationship. The technical consultant may become a "shaman" for the policy-maker, giving credibility and legitimacy to decisions.[13]

Technical consultants can be used by an agency in many ways: to define policy issues making explicit public needs, to develop the range of policy alternatives to be considered by an agency, to recommend a specific course of action or to prepare justifications for a course of action that has already been determined. When Massport hired consulting firms to assess the impact of specific projects, it was seeking justification for decisions already made. This was explicit in its work statement to the consultants describing the objectives of the environmental impact study:

> To expand previous public hearing testimony and to develop comprehensive environmental statements with appropriate supporting analyses demonstrating that: the plans for improvement of Logan have been thoroughly reviewed, . . . of the various practical alternate courses for improvement of the airport, the preferred alternate represents the best course of action from the standpoint of the effect on the environment, safety, capacity, and costs.[14]

Decisions supported by consultants may be viewed as "rational," in large measure because they are based on data provided by technical experts; the data itself are considered objective because data-gathering is directed by rational procedures. Yet "rationality" in technological planning is defined in terms of a particular set of values generally based on the assumptions that relevant costs can be expressed in dollars and that there is consensus as to the dollar value of particular impacts. The problem with these assumptions is evident as soon as decisions based on them become controversial. Those opposing a plan argue that moral and social values are neither reducible to dollars nor commensurable and so cannot be used as part of a negotiated "trade-off."[15]

Airport opponents challenged the "objective" technical basis of Massport's decisions for other reasons as well. The very gathering of data may be determined by the task that is assigned, and therefore by the questions and issues considered to be appropriate. While the quality of a consultant's work is controlled by the need to maintain his professional reputation; it is the client, in this case Massport, who defines the boundaries of the problem and instructs the consultant on the alternatives to be assessed. And just as bias can enter in the selection of pertinent data, so it can enter into its interpretation, for "neutral" facts, gathered according to professional standards, tend to be interpreted so as to be consistent with already existing beliefs and expectations.[16]

The City of Boston brought together its own experts to examine the mass of technical data supporting Massport policy, and as each consultant's report appeared the city took issue with both the data and its interpretation. In particular they pointed to omissions. When Massport consultants argued that new runways would reduce noise impact, critics observed they did not study how the new configurations would redistribute noise and affect other areas. Similarly, Massport provided evidence that, despite an increase in air traffic, new runways would increase operational flexibility. With flights diverted to over-water approaches the noise problem would decrease. Critics argued that consultants neglected to note that runway use is in large part constrained by wind direction. Nor in arguing the urgency of expansion did Massport consider the possibility of increasing flexibility by adjusting Logan's present operations. According to the Behn report, Massport's own raw data suggested that with a reasonable adjustment Logan could accommodate a 50-percent increase in actual business.[17] In 1970, for example, aircraft were operating at an average of 49-percent capacity, suggesting that fewer planes could fly more fully loaded. And scheduling or operational changes to distribute the hours of peak demand or economic controls such as landing fees to discourage peak-hour use of the runways could significantly reduce the need to expand airport capacity.

Massport critics questioned the interpretation as well as the selection of data, taking issue, for example, with the use of economic base theory as a way to estimate the indirect economic benefits of the airport. This, a city economist claimed, is misleading. "It is not the airport *per se* that is generating employment. Rather demand for air transport in the Boston metropolitan area is a fundamental source of Logan's success. And if the airport facilities were located elsewhere within the metropolitan area, they too would be successful."[18] Massport's use of data to predict future airport demand was also questioned. Projections were based on the growth pattern of the 1960s. The decrease in air travel demand in 1970 could have been regarded either as a new data point or as an anomaly. Massport chose the latter interpretation, ignoring the 1970 slump. And consultants making these projections also failed to indicate the possible variance in their estimates or to suggest that measures of variance could be useful for decision-making purposes.[19] Finally, their projections also ignored the possibility of competitive alternatives to air travel. If such projections are used as a basis for policy, critics argued, they can be self-fulfilling since continued improvement of an airport system at the expense of alternate systems can clearly perpetuate a given pattern of growth.

Given the nature of the consulting arrangement, the consultant is bound to be more sensitive to a client's interest than to the needs of opposing groups. Presenting data concerning the airport's economic impact on Boston, one consultant observed: "It is inconceivable that an enterprise of this magnitude [Massport] can be treated other than with the most profound respect."[20] What happens then, when a consultant's data are clearly detrimental to the interests of the client? The preparation of the controversial Bolt, Beranek and Newman study of Logan Airport noise suggests some of the strains that occur when consultants work on controversial issues. Several BBN researchers were sympathetic to East Boston complaints. One man systematically took photographs of airplanes, documenting those that were violating the glide path guidelines, unnecessarily exacerbating the noise problem. Various staff members proposed different solutions to the noise problem, but the scientists who worked directly on the project argued that basic community patterns of East Boston—the relationships between parents and children, the active street life—were disrupted by noise and that the situation called for major operational changes at the airport. They viewed simple solutions such as housing insulation or air-conditioning as inadequate. An internal debate took place as the directors of the consulting firm, concerned with the acceptability of the report to its sponsors and the implications of offensive findings for future contracts, sought a way to write the report in a way that would be palatable to the joint DOT-HUD sponsors.

In the end, the report presented a variety of views and included the basic facts concerning the large number of people exposed to airport noise. Even after the rewrite requested by the DOT, the sponsoring agencies refused to circulate the study until threatened with legal action, lending some credibility to the claim of airport critics that consultants were used to promote the legitimacy and acceptability of existing policy.[21]

The self-serving character of Massport's use of expertise was less the result of intent than the inevitable expression of a set of values embodied in the conception of their immediate tasks. From a different perspective, people in East Boston felt that many of the problematic issues were not matters of expertise at all. Thus, an East Bostonian responded to Massport's effort at professional evaluation of noise impact; "We need no experts. We need no medical testimony here. These people will verify themselves from personal testimony what affect noise has on the heartbeat, what affect it has on your hearing, what affect it has on your nervous system, what affect it has on your organ system."[2][2]

Threats to Autonomy

How can bureaucracies respond to demands for account-ability and public participation? Bureaucracies, especially those that are highly centralized, resist outside pressure to change. There is, suggests Anthony Downs, a tendency on the part of most officials to resist intervention and to preserve the status quo.[23] In the highly regulated air-travel industry the status quo involves many outside controls, but they are familiar and therefore not threatening. Years of collaboration between airports and regulatory agencies such as the FAA and the CAB have created certain understandings. Demands of regulatory agencies concerned specifically with safe and efficient air transportation are predictable. However, the issues raised by those concerned with noise and access problems portend less predictable regulatory arrangements. Requirements to integrate expan-sion plans with the policy of "the transportation czar" or to increase community involvement in decision-making are extraordinarily threatening. In particular, the loss of decision-making autonomy through participation of other groups implies an element of risk that to an organization like Massport is incompatible with the high priority it places on efficiency and safety. An authority does not run by consensus, argues a member of the Massport board. And so Massport seeks to maintain its power to make decisions unquestioned by outside agents. Placed increasingly on the defensive, it offers justifications for its position: its expertise, its legal and financial obligations, the "rationality" of its policy in contrast to the "emotionalism" of the opposition and, finally, its service in the public interest.

Massport tends to trivialize the opposition, considering the intervention of community leaders as "emotional" and that of elected politicians as self-serving and politically motivated. According to Director of Aviation Richard Mooney, the mayor gains by siding with voters against the airport and at the same time reaps for his city the economic benefits of Massport growth; opposing Massport carries no political risk because the economic impact of delaying airport growth will occur far in the future. Politicians, Mooney believes, should guide the judgment of people, not merely "react to hysteria."[24]

The time spent in dealing with the "annoyance" of airport opposition has rankled. "It involves going over the same material day after day and then being accused that one never provides enough information."[25] "Frankly the number of hours is just becoming impossible to satisfy all the requests for information and participation .... We have an organization that is trying to function also."[26] Some staff members regarded the governor's appointment of James Fay as chairman of the Massport board as a political means to delay decisions. An outsider on the board tends to force more time-consuming discussion of questions the staff considers irrelevant to the task at hand. The increased number of studies and committees forced by controversial questions are irritating. "It is well known," claims King, "that when one does not want to make a decision one appoints a committee to do a study."[27] To control the situation, Massport has set up its own procedures to investigate complaints, has formed new internal committees to handle such problems as community relations and has avoided giving power to committees that include outside members.

Resistance to outside interference is such that they simply would rather not hear about it. When local newspapers also began to question aspects of Massport's policies, John Thompson, then chairman of the board, wondered "if we wouldn't be better off doing away with our clipping service, to be honest with you, because I think we shouldn't pay attention to what we read in the newspapers. I think it is unfortunate for an organization important to the entire Commonwealth to see the continuing speculation as to what is going on here."[28]

One way organizations maintain autonomy is to avoid statements of long-term policy. Individual decisions by themselves may raise few questions. A policy, on the other hand, is a framework that sets the pattern for a series of decisions. It implies a long-range commitment to certain objectives and suggests the cumulative implications of single decisions. Furthermore, policy statements are particularly vulnerable to debate and criticism. The incremental changes that result from piecemeal planning are far less controversial and bureaucracies thus tend to avoid circulating long-term plans. Massport, for example, long resisted pressures to develop a comprehensive master plan that would impose future commitments and constraints and be vulnerable to attack preferring to deal with each issue according to the staff's best judgment at the time.

The lack of a master plan has been one of the most frustrating issues for airport opponents who want a coherent policy to which they can respond. Indeed, the master plan debate has been a major theme throughout the Logan Airport controversy and the focus of public demands for Massport accountability . . . . Given their scale and implications for other public expenditures, Massport decisions are in fact policies. The apparently minor decision to build a parking garage is also a policy to encourage the use of private cars and bears on the need for a third harbor tunnel. The decision to fill an area of the harbor causes environmental changes that are irreversible and determines subsequent choices concerning the use of specific areas.

For such reasons city and state government began to press Massport for a master plan during the fight over parallel runway 15-33 in 1969. They asked for a detailed analysis of short-range (to five years), middle-range (5 to 10 years) and long-range (10 to 20 years) airport development. They wanted a master plan to differentiate what was committed from what was merely proposed and to provide alternatives that included the reasoning behind given recommendations. Such a comprehensive document would provide a basis for public discussion and allow those concerned about the future of Logan to become more involved in the evaluation of projects. In Altshuler's judgment, "Just as war is too important to leave solely to the generals, Logan is too important to leave solely to Massport staff. Its development must be planned in a systematic, comprehensive, and open manner, with reasonable consideration for the views of elected officials and for the legitimate concern of their constituents."[29]

The Massport staff was extraordinarily reluctant to respond to requirements for what it called a "super master plan," claiming that it had in fact promulgated a plan as required by the FAA. This was a "layout plan"—a five-page description of current and proposed airport facilities approved by the FAA in February 1970. Logan critics, however, would not accept this, arguing that although the FAA did not require a detailed master plan as a condition for federal aid, it did recommend such a document; FAA guidelines calling for a plan that "would

satisfy aviation demands and be compatible with the
environment, community development, other modes of
transportation and other airports" sounded much like the
comprehensive statement they had long requested.[30]

Responding to pressure for a full master plan, in April
1971 the Massport board asked Executive Director King to
display such a plan at the next month's meeting. The
board was informed that there would have to be a delay of
five to eight months. Six months later, with no plan in
view, the board voted unanimously to have a plan ready to
review by February 1972. February arrived, but there was
nothing to review. Finally, in April 1972, the board
received a new layout plan but with no explanatory text.
The pressure increased over the summer when John Volpe,
following a meeting with Boston representatives, announced that he would withhold DOT funds for Logan
expansion until a "complete" master plan was made
available. Then, in October, a draft document was discussed and the staff agreed to develop further material on
economic and environmental issues. They would resubmit
the documents to the board before holding public hearings
on the new Bird Island Flats runway development. Yet,
soon after this meeting, the staff went on to schedule
hearings for March 10.

On February 5, 1973, Senators Edward Kennedy and
Edward Brooke submitted to the U.S. Senate an amendment to the Airport and Airway Development Act
specifying that no airport development project for Logan
be approved until Massport prepared a master plan dealing
with issues important to Logan's neighboring communities.
This amendment was withdrawn only when the chairman
of the Senate Commerce Committee confirmed with the
DOT that it still considered as binding, Volpe's commitment to withhold airport grant funds until the approval of
a plan. Then, in mid-February, Representatives John

Moakley and Thomas O'Neil and Senators Kennedy and Brooke cabled James Fay to request postponement of the scheduled hearings on the runway extension until the project could be considered in the context of a comprehensive policy. They recommended that local communities and state and local agencies participate in the planning process prior to a final decision on the proposed projects.

The March board meeting following these congressional communications was an angry one. Maher observed that Massport was responsible to the FAA and not to Washington senators. DeFalco attributed the source of the problem to the fact that "my two friends the U.S. Senators don't know what the hell they are talking about . . . it is inconceivable to me to think that you can predict today what fifteen years from now the impact of one runway may or may not be."[31] There were two motions on the floor. James Fay moved that he, as chairman, work with Ed King to prepare a master plan for the April board meetings. After a long debate this was defeated and Fay then moved that the board heed the congressional requests and postpone the March hearings. Thompson shifted the focus from the procedural question to Massport's competence in making reasonable assessments of environmental impacts and also to the subject of safety: "If I had one smidgeon of confidence that this matter would be heard on the merits I might support you, but unfortunately my total experience is that the merits have nothing to do with these determinations. It seems to me as we sit here and delay projects that have zero environmental impact to any reasonable person, and secondly have substantial safety aspects . . . . I think we are derelict in our duty."[32] The sense of the board was succinctly conveyed by Maher who announced that he was "sick of delays, delays, delays . . . let us go and build and get moving." The motion to delay the hearings was defeated. Held as scheduled on March 10, the hearings did nothing to resolve the growing mistrust and alienation. This indeed is the price of a situation in which a bureaucracy maintains autonomy while account-ability rests with the citizen.

9

CONCLUSION: VALUES AND PUBLIC CHOICE

Belief in technological progress has been tempered by increasing awareness of its ironies; technological improvements cause disastrous environmental problems, highways displace mass transit and destroy central cities, industrial technologies create worker alienation and, the case in point, airport expansion conflicts with city and state objectives of general urban development and environmental policy and turns neighborhoods into sonic garbage dumps. The frustrating efforts to cope with the problems of airport expansion in East Boston suggest some of the enormous difficulties involved in controlling undesirable effects of technological change. Constraints on technological planning appear to involve trade-offs that pit the elusive notion of "quality of life" against economic growth and the expectation of continued progress and prosperity.

There is by no means agreement on the means to resolve environmental problems or even on whether doing so should be a top priority. Initially welcomed as a consensus issue in contrast to the divisive problems of race and poverty, environmental reform has proved to be not only costly but politically problematic, involving considerable constraints on freedom and autonomy in crucial areas of private and public decision-making.[1] Class issues are often involved; regulations to minimize pollution may put factory workers out of jobs and zoning to preserve the environmental quality of an area may preclude low-cost housing. Thus, "the environment" is often associated primarily with middle-class concerns. Yet, the airport controversy suggests that some environmental problems directly and intolerably burden working-class neighborhoods.

Depending on their values, interests and obligations, different groups hold quite different views about the degree to which environmental considerations should constrain their decisions. Massport's reaction to the controversy over Logan Airport expansion reflects its obligations to its clients (passengers and local businesses who use air-cargo facilities) and to its constituents (the airlines and bondholders). Client groups want safe, prompt and convenient service; constituents want economic certainty and efficiency. These groups, paying costs for services rendered, form a system of exchange in which Massport is, in essence, the broker. Both groups within the exchange system have a social or economic stake in continued and unrestricted airport development.

Others outside of this exchange system pay costs, but they may receive few benefits and have quite different values and demands. East Bostonians feel they are subsidizing Logan Airport by assuming the burdens of airport activities. City and state representatives, attempting to coordinate urban planning, try to influence Massport's decisions in order to implement their own projects. National environmental groups have joined the opposition because of their general concern with environmental impacts of technological change.

The alignments in the Logan controversy have been further complicated by Massport's indirect effect on the local and regional economy. As East Bostonians have often observed, airports are designed for middle- and upper-income travellers,[2] and those dislocated by airport expansion are often of a lower class than those who benefit as passengers. Yet legislators from working-class communities outside the noise-impacted area have, paradoxically, allied themselves with Massport interests. For example, Raymond C. Rourke, chairman of the Transportation Committee in the state legislature, has opposed all antiairport measures; employment is the basic concern of his working-class constituency in Lowell. Another state representative observes, "Most of us are concerned for the long range welfare of the airport. We don't want a second class airport. I feel sorry for the people of East Boston, but that's their problem. You have to consider the good of the multitude."[3]

From one perspective, the activities of groups opposed to Logan Airport and similar movements elsewhere appear as a modern form of nineteenth century "Luddism," a wholesale rejection of technological change. Zbigniew Brzezinski has called such opposition "the death rattle of the historically obsolete,"[4] a view essentially shared by Massport when it argues the inevitability of growth. According to this view, technological growth is associated with emancipation from parochial community values, and it is considered inevitable that some parts of society will be destroyed by the basically positive forces of change.

From another perspective, protest groups are a positive and necessary force in a society that, as Theodore Roszak sees it, has "surrendered responsibility for making morally demanding decisions, for generating ideals, for controlling public authority, for safeguarding the society against its despoilers."[5] While most of us are "frozen in a position of befuddled docility," protest groups are fighting to preserve the human values lost in the course of technological progress.

But East Bostonians do not see themselves as extremists, as Luddites opposing all technological change or as utopians trying to restore some vague ideal. They argue for "justice" and basic "rights": "Does the working community have a right to exist? Do we not have the same rights that other communities consider necessary?"[6] However, the language they use against Massport *is* extreme; it reflects the intensity of their resentment and suggests the extent to which the situation has become polarized. The Authority is called an "octopus," "a sand sucker," "a monster with cancerous tentacles" out to "strangle" the community. "It is one thing to know a monster exists, but quite another to hear its roar and breathe its excrement." The images are sinister and suggest an all-pervasive, impenetrable force that grabs and totally dominates its victims. Confronted by this force East Bostonians use the language of "total war": "devastation," "battles," "jeopardy," "blitzkrieg," "physical destruction" and "moral annihilation." They call Massport's donations to their sports clubs "pacification by a dictator," and they hope to "reclaim land" and "to survive totalitarian control."[7]

Not surprisingly, Massport regards itself as benevolent. John Thompson, one-time chairman of Massport's board summarizes the public-spirited assumptions basic to the Authority's planning:

> There are a number of choices available to us today as members of society and as responsible governmental officials. We can turn away from the pressures that population put upon governmental facilities. We can ignore them and avoid planning for them. We at Massport don't think that's our function. I hear continuing discussion over the need for a balanced transportation system . . . a balanced system is simply one thing, a balancing of the countervailing interests of society to the benefit of the greatest number of people.[8]

This principle of "the greatest good for the greatest number" is commonly used by policy-makers to justify controversial decisions. Yet, as soon as one group argues that its legitimate rights are violated by practices of another this raises a profound dilemma.[9] Considerations of justice call for questioning whether any reduction in the welfare of some citizens can be justified by the greater advantages to others; whether, in the case of Logan, widespread passenger convenience or other airport benefits can warrant disregarding the daily and often excruciating discomfort of a few; whether the intensity and magnitude of costs borne by airport neighbors through the disruption of community, of schools, of sleep can be reasonably incorporated into a calculation of the "greatest good."[10] East Bostonians, in fact, have raised some of these objections:

> There are more important things in the life of the people in greater Boston than just economic growth. The Boston airport was built to serve the people. It was not constructed to make people, neighbors, schools, churches, or hospitals its servants. Our concern is not with mortar or machines. It is for the people of East Boston . . . when we have reached the point when our creations are more important than our creators, then it is time to call a stop, and we must not go on just because we call it progress.[11]

If the "greater good" principle is problematic, so is the notion of "the public interest." The concept is ambiguous, often only a euphemism for bureaucratic convenience.[12] Airport opponents regard it as such, pointing out how Massport's estimates of public needs are tied closely to its own financial needs and obligations, and the interests of a special group of airport clients and constituents. "I submit," says one East Bostonian, "that the members of the

Massachusetts Port Authority have prostituted themselves to the pursuit of the almighty dollar to the exclusion of every other consideration." And others, defining the issue as "people *or* progress," claim, "they are not interested in the people. Their great purpose and emphasis has been on progress and people be damned."[13]

The increasing opposition to airports, power plants and other large-scale public projects has called attention to inequities of technological change and the political and administrative obstacles to resolving associated social problems. Given the far-reaching and controversial consequences of such projects, market controls—the demands of clients and constituents—are insufficient to broaden the range of considerations of special-purpose bureaucracies. Their usefulness lies in their administrative and technical competence to implement accepted and coherent objectives. Assuming these objectives to be noncontroversial, they develop fixed patterns of action tied to specific technologies and a narrowly defined conception of their task. The perpetuation of such bureaucracies is linked to the promotion of this task and they tend neither to understand nor to respond to pressures to incorporate social costs as well as conventional operating costs into their calculations. Preconceptions as to the "rational" way to conduct business reinforced by ongoing interests and obligations limit consideration of available alternatives. Massport, for example, defined its task as promotion of air transportation rather than as a general responsibility to provide intercity transportation. Thus the Authority saw alternative technologies, such as high-speed rail, as a competitive problem rather than a viable substitute and rejected proposed changes in scheduling that were directed to relieving the problems of airport neighbors as outside its mandate.

Communities are increasingly aware of the desirability of protecting their local environment just as new technologies are encouraging the development of larger and more centralized facilities. How then can one balance community concerns against diffuse social and economic needs served by patterns of regional and national development? The Logan controversy and other siting disputes suggest that resolution by negotiation or "trade-off" is unlikely.[14] There are few points of agreement to serve as the basis for negotiation when the use of a particular piece of land is in dispute. Furthermore, in many technological decisions (as, for example, those involving noise) neither party can be assured that negotiated limitations will permanently be observed or that appropriate future compensations will be forthcoming. (Volpe's promise to compensate East Boston for the loss of Wood Island Park is a case in point.) And some actors in a controversy may prefer indefinite postponement to a resolution requiring compromise in order to find a mutually acceptable solution.

If negotiation seems to be futile, adjudication by the courts appears equally unpromising. In the area of civil rights there are constitutional constraints that limit sacrificing individuals for the "common good." There is no equivalent for individuals or communities that bear the costs inflicted by majority interests in technological change. While the law and its provisions for compensation are explicitly designed to keep justice from being sacrificed to efficiency, the courts are not primarily policy-making bodies.[15] Constrained to make "yes" or "no" rulings in specific situations and tending to avoid setting precedents, they often deal inadequately with general questions of "fairness."[16] Indeed, the City of Boston's failure to win a favorable judgment in its numerous lawsuits against Massport suggests that the courts are not yet the appropriate institutions to resolve such questions.

Political and legal institutions lag far behind the technologies of speed and power, and we are seeing the consequences in political turmoil. Conflicting demands for

scarce open land together with growing community consciousness will continue to complicate technological planning. The problem as suggested by the Logan Airport
controversy is one of equity and accommodation. The
challenge is to generate responsive policies of regional and
national development that are balanced by local compensation[17]—policies that are viable yet that reflect the values
and intense concerns of those who bear disproportionate
costs of technological change. Otherwise we face a dilemma in which local opposition based on mistrust of
national goals may preclude most major projects. For,
ironically, technological developments such as airports,
which are intended to improve national cohesion, can
instead lead to fragmentation and alienation.

A Note on the Program on Science, Technology, and Society

The Cornell University Program on Science, Technology, and Society is an interdisciplinary program for teaching, research, and increased public understanding. It evolved from a concern with how scientific discovery and technological innovation are changing economic and political institutions and are altering the values that influence social behavior. The program is funded by the National Science Foundation, the Sloan Foundation, the Henry Luce Foundation, and Cornell University.

This book is one of a series of studies developed within the program to provide information on the ways in which important decisions about science and technology are made. Our studies deal with specific cases selected to analyze the social implications of science and technology and the problems of controlling technological change.

Raymond Bowers
Director

NOTES

INTRODUCTION—pages 1/11

1. Orion White, Jr. and Gideon Sjoberg call this activity "mobilization politics" in "The Emerging New Politics in America," *Politics in the Post Welfare State*, ed. M.D. Hancock and Gideon Sjoberg (New York: Columbia University Press, 1972), p. 23.

2. See Robert Alford, *Bureaucracy and Participation* (Chicago: Rand McNally, 1969) and Robert Smith, *Public Authorities Special Districts and Local Government* (Washington, D.C.: Arrow Printing Service, 1964).

3. Richard Barnett, "The Twilight of the Nation State: A Crisis of Legitimacy," *The Rule of Law*, ed. Robert P. Wolff (New York: Simon Schuster, 1972), p. 222. See also Edward Shils, *The Intellectuals and the Powers* (Chicago: University of Chicago Press, 1972).

4. Robert L. Simpson, "Beyond Rational Bureaucracy," *Social Forces*, September 1972, pp. 1-7.

5. See, for example, how this pattern develops in nuclear power plant controversies in Dorothy Nelkin, *Nuclear Power and Its Critics: The Cayuga Lake Controversy* (Ithaca: Cornell University Press, 1971) and David Jopling and Stephen Gage, "The Patterns of Public Political Resistance," *Nuclear News*, March 1971, pp. 32-35. Similarly, Alan Mazur in "Social Conflict Over Technological Inno-

vation," (mimeographed) notes similarities in the development of nuclear power plant and fluoridation controversies.

6. See, for example, Joseph Sax, *Defending the Environment* (New York: Knopf, 1971).

7. According to the Jamaica Bay Environmental Study Group, 19 airports account for more than half of the 150 million passengers enplaned each year. FAA regards five of these airports as saturated and the other 14 as approaching saturation. Environmental Studies Board, National Academy of Sciences and National Academy of Engineering, *Jamaica Bay and Kennedy Airport* (Washington, D.C., USGPO 1971).

8. For discussion on why some critical issues fail to provoke political action and then suddenly become highly politicized, see Peter Bachrach and Morton Baratz, "The Two Faces of Power," *American Political Science Review* 56 (1962): 947-52 and Matthew A. Crenson, *The Unpolitics of Air Pollution* (Maryland: Johns Hopkins Press, 1971).

9. Alford. *Bureaucracy and Participation.* passim.

10. For general discussion of the problems of the pluralist structure of power in the United States see Grant McConnell, *Private Power and American Democracy* (New York: Knopf, 1966); Nelson Polsby, *Community Power and Political Theory* (New Haven: Yale University Press, 1973); Theodore Lowi, *The End of Liberalism* (New York: W.W. Norton, 1969); and Michael Lipsky, *Protest in City Politics* (Chicago: Rand McNally, 1970).

11. See discussion by Yehezkel Dror, *Public Policy Making Reexamined* (San Francisco: Chandler, 1968).

12. Thomas Reiner, "Multiple Goals Framework for Regional Planning," Papers of Regional Science Association, 26 (1971), points out that criteria of efficiency are relative to one's objectives. A policy that is efficient according to an economic model may be inefficient if the objective is social equity. See also discussion in Lewis Mainzer, *Political Bureaucracy* (Glenview, Ill.: Scott Foresman, 1973).

13. There have been many proposals to resolve this problem of institutional lag by, for example, technology assessment or an adversary system of technological decision-making. See National Academy of Science, *Technology: Processes of Assessment and Choice*, Committee on Science and Astronautics, U.S. House of Representatives, July 1969.

1. PROBLEMS OF AIRPORT DEVELOPMENT—pages 15/28

1. Michael Berger et al., *Airport Location Problems* (New York: Practicing Law Institute, 1972).

2. In 1971, for the first time in 10 years, there was an actual decline in the total number of air operations. In part, this reflected general economic trends, and, in part, the introduction of wide-bodied jets, each carrying many more passengers. (There was an 8 percent decline in air-carrier operations but only a 0.6 percent decrease in passenger enplanements in 1971). The oil shortages have at least temporarily decreased air-carrier operations, but the long-term effects are still unknown. For material on forecasts, see *Aviation Forecasts* (annual publication), August 1967, p. 49. FAA predictions are based on estimates that the GNP will increase at a long-term rate of 4.25 percent per year. Another projection is that air-passenger traffic will increase 150 percent between 1972 and 1982 requiring 390 new primary and secondary airports. By 1970, 69 percent of the commercial aircraft fleet was jet-powered and it is anticipated that 93 percent of the fleet will be jets by 1981. In addition, the general aviation fleet is increasingly converting to jets. There were 1,833 turboprops in 1969, and 9,100 are expected by 1981. The general aviation category includes, airtaxis, charter flights, business and personal aircraft. This activity has increased from 12 million flight hours in 1960 to 25.5 million flight hours in 1970 and is expected to contribute significantly to the noise problem in the future. U.S. Environmental Protection Agency, "Transportation Noise and Noise from Equipment Powered by Internal Combustion Engines," NTID 300.13 (Washington, D.C.: USGPO, December 31, 1971).

3. *Airline Pilot*, November 1972, pp. 388-89.

4. Russell Hoyt, quoted in James P. Woolsey, "Environment Issues Stunt Airport Growth," *Aviation Week and Space Technology*, November 15, 1971, p. 47.

5. Aviation Advisory Commission, *Report on the Long Range Needs of Aviation*, Washington, D.C.: USGPO, January 1, 1973.

6. "Maplin Sinking in Quicksand," *The Observer*, March 18, 1973.

7. Norman J. Glickman, "Conflict over Public Facility Location," University of Pennsylvania Regional Science Discussion paper, February 1972.

8. C.L. Ahlberg and R. Persson, "Arlanda and Märsta: Airport and Town Planning," OECD Working Document, April 4, 1973.

9. One study calculated that out of 1,000 affected households, about 200 people would complain. TRACOR, *Community Reaction to Airport Noise*, NASA Contract NASW1549, TRACOR Project 253-004, TRACOR Document No. T-70-AU-7454-U (Austin, Texas: TRACOR, September 1970) 2 volumes.

10. Karl D. Kryter, *The Effects of Noise on Man* (New York: Academic Press, 1970), p. 393.

11. Gary Lantner, "Community Opposition to Airport Development," in Series on Airport Location and Planning (Cambridge, Mass.: Department of Civil Engineering, MIT, January 1972).

12. For a discussion of the importance of third parties in the success of local protest see Michael Lipsky, *Protest in City Politics* (Chicago: Rand McNally, 1970).

13. This is the title of a 1968 report by the Committee on Environmental Quality in the Federal Council on Science and Technology.

14. This is calculated as follows:

If I_1 and I_2 are two intensities, the difference in their size (N) in decibels is:

$$N_1 = 10 \log (I_1/I_2) \, \text{dB}$$

If I_1 increases 2 fold

$$N_2 = 10 \log 2 \, (I_1/I_2) \, \text{dB}$$

$$= 10[\log 2 + \log (I_1/I_2)] \, \text{dB}$$

$$= 10[.3 + \log (I_1/I_2)] \, \text{dB}$$

$$N_2 = 3 \, \text{dB} + N_1$$

A 10-dB increase equals a 10-fold increase in sound intensity and 20 dB equals a 100-fold increase in sound intensity. Note however that human perception of sound is not linear, so that perceived increases are usually less.

15. American Speech and Hearing Association, "Noise as a Public Health Hazard," conference proceedings, June 1968, *passim*.

16. Karl D. Kryter, *The Effects of Noise on Man* (New York: Academic Press, 1970), Part III and "City Dwellers, Teenagers Face Deafness from Noise," *Congressional Quarterly Weekly Review*, April 17, 1970, p. 1035.

17. Telephone use is difficult when ambient noise is between 60 and 70 dB, and above 75 dB it is impossible. Conversation between two people six feet apart is hampered at more than 49 dB. "Jet Noise in Airport Areas: A National Solution Required," *Minnesota Law Review*, 51 (1967): 1098.

18. Environmental Studies Board, National Academy of Sciences and National Academy of Engineering, *Jamaica Bay and Kennedy Airport*, (Washington, D.C.: USGPO 1971).

19. David C. Glass and Jerome E. Singer, *Urban Stress: Experiments on Noise and Social Stressors* (New York: Academic Press, 1972) and James D. Chalupnick, ed., *Transportation Noises, a Symposium on Acceptability Criteria* (Seattle: University of Washington Press, 1970).

20. Exposure to NEF 40 is the equivalent of 200 overflights per day with a noise level of a 100 EPNdB (effective perceived noise measured in decibels), or 60 overflights per day at 105 EPNdB, or 20 overflights per day at 110 EPNdB. This technique was developed by the firm, Bolt, Beranek and Newman. See Peter Franken et al., *Aircraft Noise and Aircraft Neighbors* (Cambridge, Mass.: Bolt, Beranek and Newman, March 1970), pp. 7-10.

21. In a notorious example, the New Point Board Urban Renewal Project in Elizabeth, New Jersey, tried to develop a $4.5 million housing project close to Newark Airport. This has been the subject of a long and bitter controversy.

22. Warren H. Deem and John S. Reed, *Airport Land Needs* (Cambridge, Massachusetts: Arthur D. Little, 1966).

23. Kenneth E. Cook, "Mass Transit to Airports—an Overview," *Highway Research Record*, No. 330 (Washington, D.C.: Highway Research Board, 1970), p. 1.

24. Committee on Transportation to and from Airports, Technical Council on Urban Transportation, *Survey of Ground-Access Problems at Airports*, Reprint of the American Society of Civil Engineers (ASCE) National Meeting on Transportation Engineering, Washington, D.C., July 21-25, 1969 (Washington: ASCE, February 1969).

2. POLICIES—pages 29/44

1. A history of changing federal regulations can be found in Gordon M. Stevenson, Jr., *The Politics of Airport Noise* (Belmont, California: Duxbury Press, 1972). A history of airport location law cases is provided in Michael Berger et al., *Airport Location Problems* (New York: Practicing Law Institute, 1972).

2. FAA regulations, part 36, *Federal Register*, November 21, 1969. These rules define noise limits at various distances from the runway threshold for certification of new types of subsonic aircraft.

3. See Hugh Folk, "The Role of Technology Assessment in Public Policy," *Technology and Man's Future*, ed. A. Teich (New York: St. Martin's Press, 1972), p. 250.

4. Gideon Kanner, "Some of My Best Friends Use Airports," *California Trial Lawyer's Association Journal*, Spring 1972, pp. 305-6. Note that similar questions were raised about putting the AEC in charge of reactor safety considering its primary obligation to encourage the development of nuclear power.

5. Statement by Rep. Harley Staggers (D-W. Virginia) cited in Katherine Johnsen, "Congress Leaves Noise Control to FAA," *Aviation Week and Space Technology*, October 23, 1972, pp. 19-20.

6. Environmental Protection Agency, "The Noise Control Act of 1972—Highlights," Washington, D.C.: EPA, December 1972.

7. Department of Transportation, Federal Aviation Administration, "Procedures and Policies for Processing Airport Development Actions Affecting the Environment," Report 5050.2A, (mimeographed) December 5, 1973.

8. Ibid., p. 5. Author's italics.

9. Stuart F. Lewin, "Noise Pollution," *Law and the Municipal Ecology* (Washington, D.C.: National Institute of Municipal Law Officers, 1970), pp. 69ff.

10. American Airlines, Inc., v. Town of Hempstead, 398F2d 369 (2d Cir. 1968).

11. Stagg v. Municipal Court of Santa Monica, in Santa Monica Judicial District, 8 Cal. Rptr. 578 (App. 1969).

12. City of Burbank v. Lockheed, 71-1637, October 1972.

13. Continuing autonomy of airport operators reflects in part their liability under state laws on the taking and damaging of private property, see "Jet Noise in Airport Areas: A National Solution Required," *Minnesota Law Review* 51 (1967): 1098.

14. For an elaborated discussion of alternates see R. Weston et al., "Port Noise Complaint," *Harvard Civil Rights—Civil Liberties Law Review* 6 (December 1970): 61-118. Also see OECD working documents for conference on April 4, 1973.

15. Effective perceived noise in decibels is a unit which, in addition to loudness (dB), accounts for pure sound components and duration.

16. Quoted in William Gregory, "Engine Noise Antidotes Weighted," *Aviation Week and Space Technology*, February 14, 1973, p. 53.

17. James P. Woolsey, "FAA Noise Paper May Ask JT8D Retrofit Program." *Aviation Week and Space Technology*, October 18, 1971, pp. 23-24.

18. U.S. Environmental Protection Agency, "Economic Impact of Noise," NTID 300:1, Washington, D.C., December 31, 1971, p. 36. A 1972 study of Arthur D. Little projected retrofit costs as follows:

Retrofit Cost Per Aircraft	707/ DC-8	727	737/ DC-9
Nacelle/Jet Supressor Kit	$0.6-0.8M	$0.6-0.8M	$0.4-0.6M
New Front Fan & Nacelle Kit	$1.2-2.0M	$1.0-1.8M	$0.8-1.4M

SOURCE: Arthur D. Little, Internal Memorandum to Logan Airport Noise Abatement Committee, 1972.

19. Aviation Advisory Commission, *Report on the Long Range Needs of Aviation*, Washington, D.C.: USGPO, January 1, 1973.

20. Note that in Japan air transportation carried 22 percent of the total passengers between Tokyo and Osaka in 1964. In 1972, with the Tokaido line, the air travel share of this route was reduced to 10 percent of the total number of travellers. *Environment* 1 (April 1973): 6-10.

21. *Washington Post*, April 18, 1966.

22. Alan Carlin and R.E. Park, "Marginal Cost Pricing of Airport Runway Capacity," *American Economic Review* 60 (June 1970): 310ff.

23. Boston *Globe*, September 8, 1972.

24. "Judge Denies Airport Petitions," *Aviation Week and Space Technology*, January 17, 1972, p. 28.

25. Indiana Toll Road Commission v. Jankovich, 379 U.S. 897,

85 S ct. 493, LEd. 2d/439, 1965. See discussion in Warren N. Deem and John S. Reed, *Airport Land Needs* (Cambridge, Mass.: A.D. Little, 1966).

26. Bolt, Beranek and Newman, "Insulation from Aircraft Noise," estimates that effective noise insulation a house with light exterior walls would cost from $400 to $4,500. If all four million homes affected by aircraft noise were covered, the cost could be as high as 20 billion dollars, clearly economically unviable.

27. Robert A. Baron, *The Tyranny of Noise* (New York: St. Martins Press, 1970).

28. United States v. Causby 328 U.S. (1946).

29. E.G. Griggs v. Alleghany County, 363 U.S. 84 (1962) and see discussion in Weston, "Port Noise Complaint."

30. James Hildebrand, "Noise Pollution," *Columbia Law Review* 70 (April 1970): 683ff.

3. LOGAN INTERNATIONAL AIRPORT—pages 47/62

1. Maurice Tobin, "Annual Message," *Addresses to the General Court* Boston, 1945-46, p. 145.

2. Massachusetts Port Authority Enabling Act, 1956, Chapter 91, p. 118.

3. Runways are numbered according to magnetic compass bearings divided by 10. Thus a runway lying due north would be 0 or 36. Runway 4 would lie at a 40-degree angle from north. R and L indicate right and left.

4. This is Massport's own calculation based on the number of "passenger enplanements," in 1971. "Enplanements" mean the number of passengers boarding flights. When airport operators refer to total numbers of passengers serviced by an airport (e.g., enplanements and deplanements) they derive the figure by doubling the number of enplanements. "Airport operations" refer to the number of planes using the airport, a number that may vary according to whether or not it includes those which use the control tower but do not land.

5. See Robert Behn, chairman, Governor's Task Force on Inter-City Transportation, "Report to Governor Sargent," April 1971, p. 83. The early projections based on 1969 data were made at the

Corps of Engineers hearing in February 1971; the second set of projections appeared in May 1971 and included 1970 data.

6. Massport *Annual Report*, Boston, 1968.

7. Richard E. Mooney, "Boston-Logan International Airport," *Airport World*, June 1969, p. 9.

8. ABT Associates, "Air Transportation for Boston, 1970-1990," January 1970, p. 80.

9. Logan is estimated to consume about 500,000 gallons of fuel daily. For each 1,000 gallons of fuel consumed by aircraft, the following pollutants are discharged: carbon monoxide, 56 lbs.; hydrocarbons, 15 lbs.; nitrogen oxide, 37 lbs.; dirt particles, 54 lbs.; aldehydes, 6 lbs. More than a third of the particulates caused by transportation in the Boston metropolitan area come from aircraft, and in 1970 carbon monoxide levels in East Boston were 13.2 parts per million, 4.2 parts over federal standards. For detailed information on aircraft emissions see U.S. Environmental Protection Agency, *Aircraft Emissions: Impact on Air Quality and Feasibility of Control* (Washington, D.C., U.S. Government Printing Office, 1973).

10. Richard E. Mooney, personal interview, October 1972.

11. Testimony by Alderman Charles DeIorio (Chelsea) and Lawrence DiCara (Dorchester) at United States Corps of Engineers, *Hearings* on Massport application for a permit to fill Boston Harbor, Boston, February 26, 1971, pp. 223, 409.

12. Robert G. Smith, *Public Authorities, Special Districts, and Local Government* (Washington, D.C.: Arrow Printing Service, 1964), *passim* for a detailed study of the structure of public authorities.

13. Ibid., p. 197.

14. Quoted from "Atlantic" in Melvin R. Levin and Norman A. Abend, *Bureaucrats in Collision: Case Studies in Area Transportation Planning* (Cambridge: MIT Press, 1971), p. 66.

15. The bond issues were as follows: 1959—$72,000,000; 1964—$106,000,000; 1969—$62,000,000; 1971—$78,000,000; 1973—$107,000,000.

16. See discussion in Chester Hartman et al., "The Massachusetts Port Authority; Public Purpose and Public Accountability," (mimeographed) May 1970.

17. Edward King, personal interview, October 4, 1972. See

similar statements in Massport's *Annual Reports*.

18. Report of the Special Commission on the Massachusetts Port Authority, 1956, quoted in Charles J. Friedman, "The Massachusetts Port Authority and the Neighboring Community," (Harvard College Honors Thesis, March 1970), p. 58.

4. "EAST BOSTON IS NOT AN AIRPORT"—pages 63/79

1. The population of East Boston has declined as follows: 1950—51,152; 1960—43,809; 1965—39,792; 1970—38,900; 1973—37,404. Much of this decline reflects the encroachment of transportation facilities including the harbor tunnel and access roads, the mass-transit system and the airport.

2. Herbert Gans, *The Urban Villagers* (New York: The Free Press, 1962), p. 163. See also S.M. Miller and Frank Riessman, "Working Class Subcultures," *Social Problems* 9 (1961): 91ff.

3. East Boston Little City Hall was set up by Mayor Kevin White in July 1968 as the first effort to decentralize city government and to provide city services to local communities. It is a large white trailer parked in the middle of Maverick Square, staffed with bilingual aides who advise community people on problems relating to housing, jobs, social security and rent control.

4. Edith DeAngelis, from testimony at United States Corps of Engineers, "Hearings on Massport application for a permit to fill three areas of Boston Harbor," Boston, February 26, 1971, p. 364 (hereafter cited as *Hearings*).

5. Mary Ellen Welch, *Hearings*, p. 347.

6. Boston's Mayor James Curley, "Speech on the 'Matera Plan' " (mimeographed) August 29, 1946.

7. Peter A. Franken et al., *Aircraft Noise and Aircraft Neighbors* (Cambridge, Massachusetts: Bolt, Beranek and Newman, March 1970).

8. TRACOR, "Community Reaction to Airport Noise," NASA Contract NASW 1549, September 1970.

9. Unless otherwise indicated, the statements from East Boston residents that appear in the rest of this chapter were collected in a residential survey made by Massachusetts Attorney General Robert H. Quinn. The survey, examining subjective responses from those

who claimed to be affected by aircraft noise, with the intention of guiding activities of the State Division of Environmental Protection, was made available to this author through the courtesy of the attorney general's office.

10. State Representative Emanuel Serra in *Hearings*, p. 189.

11. Myron S. Weinberg, president, Foster D. Snell, Inc. (a consulting firm), *Hearings*, p. 82.

12. Mark Fried and Peggy Gleicher, "Some Sources of Residential Satisfaction in an Urban Slum," *Environment in the Social Sciences*, ed. Joachim Wohlwill and Daniel H. Carson (Washington, D.C.: American Psychological Association, 1972). For similar findings in a British setting see Michael Young, *Family and Kinship in East London* (London: Penguin, 1967).

13. *East Boston Community News*, April 1, 1971.

14. *East Boston Community News*, September 12, 1972.

15. Ibid., September 26, 1972.

16. Ibid., January 16, 1973.

17. Eleanor Welch, "Observations from Neptune Road," *East Boston Community News*, May 9, 1972.

5. PLANS AND PROTESTS—pages 80/101

1. This discussion of the early history of Massport projects has benefited from several student research papers; Charles Friedman's, "The Massachusetts Port Authority and the Neighboring Community" (Harvard College honors thesis, March 1970) and Diana Brown and Stephen Kersten's, "East Boston and the Massachusetts Port Authority," (mimeographed) Harvard University, July 1972.

2. *Boston Herald Traveller*, August 25, 1966.

3. John Volpe, "Speech to Senate and House of Representatives," Commonwealth of Massachusetts, House 4082, December 5, 1966.

4. Described by Mary Ellen Welch in *East Boston Community News*, April 10, 1973.

5. Friedman, "The Massachusetts Port Authority."

6. Robert D. Johnson and Murray D. Segal.

7. Quoted in *Boston Globe*, March 25, 1969.

8. Described in Alan Lupo, Frank Colcord and Edmund Fowler,

Rites of Way: The Politics of Transportation in Boston and the U.S. City (Boston: Little Brown, 1971), pp. 35ff.

9. Ibid., p. 37.

10. Two and one-half years later in August 1972, Reverend Albert Sallese pointed out at a board meeting that this had not yet been done.

11. ABT Report, "Air Transportation for Boston, 1970-1990," January 1970, p. 80.

12. David F. Cahn et al., "Project Bosporus," Student project in Systems Engineering at Massachusetts Institute of Technology, MIT Report 21 (Cambridge, Massachusetts, 1970).

13. Committee Report on the Boston Metropolitan Airport System 1970-1990, June 1970. The Inter-Agency Committee included members from Metropolitan Area Planning Council, Massachusetts Port Authority, Department of Public Works, Massachusetts Aeronautics Commission, Massachusetts Department of Commerce, MBTA and the Department of Transportation.

14. Metropolitan Area Planning Council, Statement in Inter-Agency Committee Report, pp. 141ff.

15. Landrum and Brown, *Boston Logan International Airport Environmental Impact Statement*, 2 volumes, May 1971. The report indicates that if the runway were not built, anticipated delay by 1975 would be 8,850 hours annually costing $2,350,000.

16. Massport Authority, "Environmental Statement to the Department of Army, Corps of Engineers," (mimeographed), February 24, 1971, p. 6.

17. Testimony by Councillor Alfred O'Neill, *Hearings*, p. 217.

18. Landrum and Brown, *Boston Logan International Airport*.

19. Letter from David Standley (Boston Air Pollution Control Commission) to John McCarthy (MAPC), June 28, 1971.

20. Massachusetts Port Authority, "Responses to Environmental Comments, Outer Taxiway Project," February 10, 1972, p. 20.

21. Ibid., p. 37.

22. Landrum and Brown, "Environmental Impact Analysis for Outer Taxiway Project," February 11, 1972.

23. Landrum and Brown, "Preliminary Environmental Impact Report for Extension of Runways 4L and 9, and Construction of STOL/GA Runway 15-33," December 1972.

24. *Boston Globe*, March 7, 1973.

25. Landrum and Brown, *Boston Logan International Airport*, p. 76.

26. The new international terminal (north side) is planned with a small parking lot, somewhat removed from the main terminal. Eastern was allowed to build a completely separate terminal with a rooftop multilevel garage. There has been some criticism of the isolation of Eastern passengers who choose to use that garage. Transferring to other terminals is difficult for the only connection is a shuttle bus, on a 10-20 minute schedule. American Airlines, the principal occupant of the proposed new south terminal, wanted the same arrangement as Eastern despite concern with the problem of isolation.

27. Statement at Massachusetts Port Authority, Meeting of the Board of Directors (mimeographed transcript), December 16, 1971, pp. 8, 12.

28. Ibid., December 2, 1971, p. 85. The logic of this argument is systematically analyzed by Fred Kahn, "The Tyranny of Small Decisions," *Kyklos* 19 (1966).

29. Ibid., December 16, 1971, p. 70.

30. Ibid., December 2, 1971, p. 39.

31. Ibid., May 18, 1972, pp. 7ff.

32. Edith DeAngeles in ibid., August 10, 1972, p. 136.

6. INTERVENTIONS—pages 105/126

1. Statement in *Boston Globe*, November 26, 1972.

2. Only a small fraction of these people (333) are directly employed by Massport.

3. Loschi v. Massachusetts Port Authority, 354 Mass. 53 (1968).

4. City of Boston v. Massachusetts Port Authority, 320 7 Supp. 1317 September 12, 1970. Affirmed at 444 F2d 167.

5. City of Boston v. John Volpe et al. 464 F2d 254, July 17, 1972. Two days before oral agreement on the motion for injunction, the court's clerk told the city attorney that one of the three judges on the case owned Massport bonds, but that his broker had declared that the outcome of the case would not affect the security of the

bonds. The judge decided not to withdraw and neither the city nor the federal defendants objected.

6. City of Boston v. Massachusetts Port Authority, Suffolk Superior Court, case 97085, May 2, 1973.

7. City of Boston v. Massachusetts Port Authority, 255, Northeast Reporter 2d 597, February 3, 1970.

8. John W. Giorgia, "Parklands and Federally Funded Highway Projects: The Impact of *Conservation Society* v. *Texas*," *Environmental Affairs*, 1 (March 1972): 893-94.

9. Silva v. Romney, Docket number 72-1352, February 2, 1973.

10. Francis Sargent, interview on WEEI "Bay State Forum," April 21, 1972.

11. Currently only about five percent of airport users are served by the MBTA, one of Massachusetts' more unfortunate public authorities. Its deficit for the calendar year 1972 was $93 million, of which the state will bear about $19 million and the localities the remainder. The MBTA is run by an advisory board representing 79 cities and towns, each committed to minimizing local costs. And it negotiates separate contracts with 27 unions. (It is rumored that it costs the same per mile to run an MBTA bus as a DC9.) As it is organized now, it is unlikely that use of the MBTA for airport access will increase. The line serving the airport terminates at City Hall and is thus relatively inconvenient for passengers from suburbs or other parts of Boston. And at the airport end, the station is a mile from the terminals, requiring a shuttle service.

12. Robert Behn, chairman, Governor's Task Force on Inter-City Transportation, "Report to Governor Sargent," April 1971, p. ii.

13. Speech at regional meeting of Metropolitan Area Planning Council. Press release from governor's office, Boston, July 8, 1971.

14. The decision to build a special tunnel was also tied to attempts to block the construction of the I-95 north expressway which was not feasible without a general-purpose tunnel. Thus, while antihighway forces were reluctant to support a tunnel because they sympathized with the East Boston concern about airport expansion, they did not obstruct the governor's plan.

15. Martin Coughlin quoted in *East Boston Community News*, July 18, 1972.

16. Francis W. Sargent and Alan A. Altshuler, "Transportation and Construction: Reorganization Recommendations," Phase II (mimeographed), Boston, January 1973.

17. Quoted in *Boston Globe*, December 11, 1971.

18. *Boston Globe*, December 31, 1971.

19. *Boston Globe*, December 17, 1971.

20. Environmental Studies Board, National Academy of Sciences and National Environmental Studies Board, National Academy of Sciences and National Academy of Engineering, *Jamaica Bay and Kennedy Airport*, (Washington, D.C.: USGPO 1971).

21. Massachusetts Port Authority, *Meeting of the Board of Directors* (transcript), July 20, 1972, pp. 63-64 (hereafter referred to as *Board Meeting*).

22. Quoted in *Boston Globe*, January 18, 1973.

23. *Boston Globe*, January 25, 1973.

24. The governor also proposed that if a vacancy on the board became available and he chose not to make a new appointment within 30 days, and if there were no more than three members of the governor's party on the board, then the secretary of transportation would automatically become an *ex-officio* member of the board. This approach is based on constitutional restrictions; no individual in Massachusetts can hold more than two gubernatorial appointments at the same time so that the secretary could not be appointed as a regular member of several boards.

25. House Bill 5387.

26. *Board Meeting*, February 17, 1972, p. 39.

27. Ibid., p. 46. Note that later, in October 1973, the Massport board voted that by 1979 Massport would impose a fine on all commercial jets that violated FAA noise standards. This would require jets using Logan to refit their engines.

28. *Board Meeting*, March 9, 1972, pp. 51-56.

29. House Bill 5387, March 29, 1972, p. 11.

30. William Lyden at *Board Meeting*, April 20, 1972, pp. 141-42.

31. In 1970, the primary lobbyist William Malloy was paid $22,000 to represent Massport. Two other men earned $13,000 a piece. In January 1973, Malloy's salary was raised to $26,000.

32. Michael Dukakis, "Report and Recommendations on the Massachusetts Port Authority," (mimeographed) November 26, 1971.

33. See R. Weston et al., "Port Noise Complaint," *Harvard Civil Rights—Civil Liberties Law Review* December 1970, p. 101.

34. Edward Maher at *Board Meeting*, February 17, 1972, p. 113.

7. Placations   —pages 127/139

1. Massachusetts Port Authority, Meeting of the Board of Directors, (transcript) June 15, 1972, p. 26 (hereafter referred to as *Board Meeting*).

2. The brochure was reprinted from a transcript of a WNAC-TV talk by Robert Gilbertson.

3. Reported by Fred Salvucci, personal interview, May 8, 1973. In 1972, the Massachusetts Aeronautics Commission received 749 noise complaints about Logan Airport.

4. *East Boston Community News*, December 5, 1972.

5. Newsome & Company, "Public Relations Study prepared for Massachusetts Port Authority," Boston, November 1972, p. II-5.

6. Ibid., p. ii.

7. Edward King, personal interview, October 1972.

8. *Board Meeting*, February 17, 1972, p. 40.

9. Ibid., pp. 51, 54.

10. *Board Meeting*, May 18, 1972, pp. 42, 43.

11. Ibid., p. 44.

12. *Board Meeting*, August 10, 1972, p. 48.

13. *Board Meeting*, June 15, 1972, p. 19.

14. *Board Meeting*, April 20, 1972, p. 14.

15. *Board Meeting*, February 17, 1972, p. 8.

16. *Board Meeting*, August 10, 1972, p. 16.

17. Ibid., p. 63.

18. Neil Lynch, Massport Attorney, *Board Meeting*, January 19, 1973.

8. CHALLENGES TO AUTHORITY—pages 143/162

1. See the discussion in Dennis F. Thompson, *The Democratic Citizen* (Cambridge: Cambridge University Press, 1970) and Robert Alford, *Bureaucracy and Participation* (Chicago: Rand McNally, 1969).

2. This term was suggested by Irving Louis Horowitz. This response of territorial protection, of trying to control neighborhood problems, is one of several alternatives for the citizen who can resign himself to a situation, or leave. The conditions fostering these

responses are analyzed by Albert O. Hirschman, *Exit, Voice and Loyalty: Response to Decline in Firms, Organizations and States* (Cambridge: Harvard University Press, 1970) and John M. Orbell and Toru Uno, "A Theory of Neighborhood Problem Solving: Political Action vs. Residential Mobility," *American Political Science Review*, June 1972, pp. 471-89.

3. Gerald O'Leary (councillor), testimony, U.S. Corps of Engineers, "Hearings on the Application by the Massachusetts Port Authority for a permit to fill three areas of Boston Harbor," Boston, February 26, 1971, p. 212 (hereafter cited as *Hearings*).

4. Carol Pateman, *Participation and Democratic Theory* (Cambridge: Cambridge University Press, 1970).

5. Sister Margaret Pierce, testimony in *Hearings*, p. 411.

6. Stanley Oborsky, testimony in *Hearings*, pp. 421-22.

7. Quoted in *Boston Globe*, October 21, 1972. Specifically with reference to antihighway activist.

8. Massachusetts Port Authority, Meeting of the Board of Directors, August 10, 1972, pp. 99-106 (hereafter cited as *Board Meeting*).

9. Reverend Marshall Bevins, testimony at *Hearings*, p. 282.

10. Governor Sargent, *Board Meeting*, December 16, 1971, p. 6.

11. The problems of resources and expertise available to citizens' groups are discussed by Marvin Manheim et al., "Community Values in Highway Location and Design: A Procedural Guide," Urban Systems Laboratory, M.I.T. report No. 71-4, Boston, September 1971. In another area, see John W. Gofman and Arthur R. Tamplin *Poisoned Power*, ch. 12, (Emmaus, Pennsylvania: Rodale Press, 1971). See also Philip Bereano, "The Scientific Community and the Crisis of Belief," *American Scientist* 57 (1969): 484-501.

12. Edward King, testimony at *Hearings*, p. 101.

13. Norton E. Long, "Public Policy and Administration: The Goals of Rationality and Responsibility," *Public Administration Review* 14, (1954): 22.

14. Massachusetts Port Authority, "Work Statement, Environmental Impact Study," April 16, 1971, p. 2. Robert Behn suggested the wide range of possible consulting arrangements.

15. See discussion by Lawrence Tribe in "Policy Science: Analysis or Ideology," *Philosophy and Public Affairs* 2 (Fall 1972): 66-110.

16. See discussion by Larston R. King and Philip H. Melanson, "Knowledge and Politics," *Public Policy*, Winter 1972, pp. 83-101.

17. Robert Behn, chairman, Governor's Task Force on Inter-City Transportation, "Report to Governor Sargent," April 1971, p. 83. This kind of adjustment would depend, of course, on the cooperation of the airlines and the CAB.

18. City of Boston, departmental communication to Robert Weinberg, comments on Massport consultants report, June 23, 1971.

19. Robert Behn, personal communication, 1973.

20. Landrum and Brown, "Environmental Impact Analysis for Outer Taxiway Project," Massport Consultants Project, February 11, 1972, pp. IX-3.

21. In 1968 the FAA also tried to avoid distributing the "Baxter Report," a study of the legal aspects of noise that recommended that the industry internalize the costs of noise.

22. Mario Umana, testimony at U.S. Corps of Engineers, "Hearings on Massport for a permit to fill three areas of Boston Harbor," Boston, February 26, 1971, pp. 131-32. The ultimate expression of this sentiment was given by Vice-President Spiro Agnew, responding to the report by the United States Presidential Commission on Pornography and Obscenity: "I don't care what the experts say, I know pornography corrupts."

23. In a study of bureaucracies, Anthony Downs explains the tendency toward continued expansion; growth attracts more capable personnel, provides leadership with increased prestige and power, reduces internal conflict and improves chances for economic survival. Anthony Downs, *Inside Bureaucracy* (Boston: Little Brown, 1967).

24. Richard Mooney, personal interview, October 1972.

25. Ibid.

26. John Thompson, statement at *Board Meeting*, February 17, 1972.

27. Edward King, personal interview, October 1972.

28. *Board Meeting*, July 20, 1972, p. 63.

29. Statement on behalf of Governor Sargent at a public hearing, conducted by Massport, (mimeographed) March 10, 1973.

30. In particular the FAA called for plans for long-term planning based on advice from "private citizens, community organizations, airport users, area-wide planning agencies, conservation groups,

ground transit offices, and aviation and airport concessionaire interests" and emphasized the need for coordination with other planning bodies. DOT, FAA Advisory booklet on Airport Master Plans," AC 150/5070-6, February 1971

31. *Board Meeting*, March 1, 1973, pp. 31-32.

32. Ibid., p. 133.

9. CONCLUSION: VALUES AND PUBLIC CHOICE—pages 163/170

1. For discussion of some of the problems of environmental reform see Denton E. Morrison et al., "The Environmental Movement," in *Social Behavior, Natural Resources and The Environment*, eds. William Burch et al. (New York: Harper & Row, 1972).

2. In 1963, New York domestic passengers had a median income of $15,000 as contrasted with the median income of $6,190 in the United States adult population as a whole. See discussion in James R. Nelson, "The Value of Travel Time," in *Problems in Public Expenditure Analysis*, ed. Samuel B. Chase (Washington, D.C.: Brookings Institute, 1968).

3. Quoted anonymously in Newsome & Company, "Public Relations Study Prepared for Massachusetts Port Authority," Boston, November 1972, chap. VI, p. A-29.

4. Zbigniew Brzezinski, "America and the Technetronic Age," *Between Two Ages: America's Role in the Technetronic Era* (New York: Viking, 1970).

5. Theodore Roszak, *The Making of a Counter Culture* (New York: Doubleday, 1968), p. 22.

6. Emanuel Serra, state representative, testimony, U.S. Corps of Engineers, "Hearings on the Application by the Massachusetts Port Authority for a permit to fill three areas of Boston Harbor," Boston, February 26, 1971, p. 189 (hereafter cited as *Hearings*). Richard Sennett and Jonathan Cobb describe "the sense of injured dignity" prevalent in working-class communities of ethnic origin in *The Hidden Injuries of Class* (New York: Knopf, 1972).

7. This language is used in public hearings, newspaper statements, editorials, etc. See, for example, *East Boston Community News*, September 26, 1972.

8. John Thompson, testimony at *Hearings*, p. 28.

9. See discussion of the problem of the "tyranny of the majority" in Robert Dahl, *A Preface to Democratic Theory* (Chicago: University of Chicago Press, 1956). Also note the conception of justice formulated by John Rawls, *A Theory of Justice* (Cambridge: Harvard University Press, 1971). Rawls considers it unjust to "allow the sacrifices imposed on a few [to be] outweighed by the larger sum of advantages enjoyed by many," (p. 4) and that "the principle of utility is incompatible with the . . . idea of reciprocity implicit in a notion of a well-ordered society" (p. 14).

10. The need to incorporate intensity of preference into decisions are discussed by Wilmore Kendall and George Carey, "The Intensity Problem and Democratic Theory," *American Political Science Review* 62 (March 1968): 5-24 and Dennis Mueller, "Constitutional Democracy and Social Welfare," *Quarterly Journal of Economics* 87 (February 1973): 60-80.

11. Congressman Thomas O'Neill, testimony at *Hearings*, p. 171.

12. Glendon Schubert, *Public Interest* (New York: Free Press, 1961).

13. Robert Gagin and Monsignor Mimie Pitaro (state representative) testimony at *Hearings*, pp. 153, 270.

14. Mary Douglas in "Environments at Risk," *Times Literary Supplement*, (October 30, 1970) discusses the different moral consensus involved in environmental disputes and the fact that it is unlikely that one side can impose its values on the other.

15. Frank I. Michelman, "Property, Utility and Fairness: Comments on the Ethical Foundations of Just Compensation Law," *Harvard Law Review* 80 (April 1967): 1226.

16. Ibid., p. 1251. Michelman makes this point in discussing compensation law.

17. A discussion of compensatory schemes can be found in Federal Aviation Administration, "Community Values in the Planning and Evaluation of Airport Development Projects," Report No. FAA-AV-72-2, Washington, D.C., January 1972.

INDEX

193

Index